How to Go to Work
on Your Faith

How to Go to Work on Your Faith

10 Tips for Being a Vital Christian on the Job

JERRY RAMEY
with
ED STEWART

BEACON HILL PRESS OF KANSAS CITY
KANSAS CITY, MISSOURI

Copyright 1992
by Beacon Hill Press of Kansas City

ISBN: 083-411-4305

Printed in the
United States of America

Cover Design: Paul Franitza

10   9   8   7   6   5   4   3   2   1

Contents

Introduction		7
1	Jump into the Job with Both Feet	13
2	Try Hard to Be Number Two	26
3	Leave the Status Quo Behind	38
4	Be Ready When Murphy Strikes	51
5	Hold Your Values Together	63
6	Remain True to the Truth	73
7	Give Till It Helps	84
8	Let Bygones Be Bygones	96
9	Keep an Open Mind	108
10	Make Everyone Feel like Number One	120

Introduction

Getting the Trust and Respect You Deserve;
Deserving the Trust and Respect You Get

Zack was a field representative for Tektronix Corporation who lived in Boston and occasionally visited Tek's main plant in Portland, Oreg., where I worked for 23 years. Whenever Zack came to town, I would chat with him at meetings and coffee breaks about work-related issues. My relationship with Zack was casual, but friendly and positive.

On one of my frequent business trips to Boston I ran into Zack in a hotel one evening. He invited me to join him for dinner, and as we ate together, we caught up on the latest company news. I'm not sure how it happened, but the conversation eventually turned to the topic of Christianity. "My wife is a Christian, but she has a little too much religious fervor for me," Zack disclosed wryly. "You're a Christian, too, aren't you, Jerry?"

I was surprised by Zack's observation because we had never talked about matters of faith before. "Yes I am, Zack," I admitted. "How did you know?"

"I just had a feeling about you," Zack answered. "I guess it's from watching the way you've dealt with engineering and handled some of the frustrations with the sales organization."

For the next couple of hours I shared with Zack what Jesus Christ means in my life and in my work. I didn't preach to him; I simply told him that I was committed to Christ and to being an authentic Christian in everything I do, including my career. Zack was open and inquisitive, and I was privileged to share with him some of the wonderful things God has done in my life.

"I want to hear more about your relationship with

Jesus," Zack told me before we parted that night. He invited me to his home for dinner the next time I was in Boston. As we said good-bye, I knew God was going to do something special in Zack's life.

A few months later I was in Boston again, and I took Zack up on his invitation. When Zack, his wife, Geri, and their two children met me at the door of their home, I sensed excitement in the air. They couldn't wait to tell me their story.

"The night Zack was at the hotel with you," Geri began, "I was at a Bible study meeting. The Lord touched me during that meeting in a special way—but I didn't know why. I just thanked Him for His blessing and went home."

"Geri was still awake when I got home," Zack picked up the story. "When I told her about our conversation, she told me about the sense of God's blessing she felt at her Bible study meeting. As Geri and I talked about God that night, He was right there with us, Jerry—I know He was! Geri and I got down on our knees, and I asked Jesus to take complete control of my life."

I was ecstatic! I had played a part in seeing Zack move into a total commitment to Christ, and his family was now a vibrant Christian family.

I had a similar experience with Trevor, a man I worked for at Tek. Trevor's day-to-day conversation revealed to me that he was actively searching for meaning in his life. For nine months Trevor asked me questions about my life as a Christian. "Your work and your attitude display your beliefs," Trevor finally admitted one day. I had the privilege of praying with Trevor when he opened his life to Jesus.

Before you get the wrong idea, you must know that my experiences of helping Zack and Trevor find Christ were rare spiritual highlights in my 23-year history as an employee at Tektronix. No, I didn't have a stream of coworkers filing into my office each week to hear my testimony and kneel to receive Christ. I didn't sponsor a lunch-hour Bible study in order to share the gospel with my fellow employees. I didn't even invite many of them to go to church with me. There's nothing wrong with any of these outreach activities, but that just isn't my style. I'm a Christian businessman, not an evangelist.

But even though I don't see myself as one who is gifted in evangelism, I do understand that—along with you and every other Christian—I am called by God to be a witness for Jesus Christ wherever I am. And like the majority of Christians who spend approximately 40 hours each week working in some arena of gainful employment, the primary recipients of my witness are my fellow employees. Tektronix was my main mission field for 23 years. Today my missionary endeavors are divided between a couple of small companies where I am one of the senior partners. And the place where you work is your main mission field. Most of us spend more time in the company of our coworkers than with any other group of people outside our families, including our Christian friends. If we are not authentic, attractive witnesses for Christ in our places of employment, any attempts at "witnessing" elsewhere are hollow and contrived.

I firmly believe that only 5 percent of our witness in the world consists of what we say; but 45 percent is what we do, and 50 percent is how we do it. As a result, my witnessing goal as a Christian on the job has been to draw my coworkers to Christ by my actions without verbally buttonholing them. I am committed to letting people know that I am a Christian and to demonstrating my Christian spirit and values without being preachy or offensive. Our coworkers are not as interested in hearing the gospel from us as in seeing the gospel in us. Our words about Christ may or may not be heard and received. But our Christlike attitudes and actions, demonstrated in the pressures, conflicts, and crises of the daily work environment, will always make a positive impact on our unbelieving coworkers.

Yes, I know that sharing the gospel with people must eventually include a verbal presentation of Christ. We cannot expect people to receive Jesus if we don't verbalize that He is the Point of Origin behind our positive attitudes and actions. That's why I like to keep one or two simple, clear scriptures or poignant quotes in view next to my desk. And that's why I'm not afraid to talk about how God is working in my life or to reveal that I pray to Him and depend on Him to help solve my problems at work. But the critical 5 percent of our witnessing words must be securely founded on the supercritical 95 percent of our witnessing deeds and attitudes, which make our words, when we are able to speak them, credible. When people see the substance of Christian values consistently portrayed in our behavior, they'll know who to come to when they want to talk.

I see two foundational pillars upon which our witnessing words must rest if they are to be believed by our coworkers. The first pillar is respect. We must gain the respect of our fellow workers if we expect them to open their hearts to us and to our verbal witness. That means that Christian employees can't be just average workers, putting in their time, doing as little work as possible, using every angle to make the system work to their advantage. We must conduct ourselves on the job in such a way that our unbelieving coworkers will respect us for our personal integrity and quality of work. When people respect us, they are more likely to seek us out when they have a need.

The second pillar is trust. We must earn the trust of our fellow workers if we expect them to welcome our witness. We will earn their trust when they perceive that we genuinely care for them. That means we can't participate in the character degradation, hurtful gossip, and selfish infighting that often characterize a staff of coworkers. Instead, we must show ourselves to be friends and helpers, not rivals or enemies. When people trust us, they will listen to what we have to say.

In addition to my experience with Zack and Trevor, I have had numbers of fellow employees come to me over the years seeking advice for their work situations and personal problems. Sometimes they just need someone to listen to them. Sometimes they want advice. Since I have endeavored to gain the respect and earn the trust of my fellow workers,

I am often able to counsel them, pray with them, and share Christ with them.

That's what this book is all about: how to gain the respect and earn the trust of your coworkers so that the words you share with them about Christ will be easily received. Each chapter deals with a quality of Christian behavior that can be specifically applied to your work environment. My prayer is that as you diligently and faithfully focus on these qualities, you will discover that your opportunities for verbal witness among your coworkers will increase—and the opportunities will be fruitful.

· 1 ·

Jump into the Job with Both Feet

AS A BOY OF 14, one of my first real paying jobs was doing assorted chores on a neighboring farm in my hometown of Salem, Oreg. That summer, our neighbor needed somebody to stack bales of hay in his field for pickup. He asked me if I could do the job in one day—for the impressive sum of $5.00! I had only bucked hay once before, but it looked like easy money to me. So I eagerly agreed.

I started at 6:30 A.M., energetically wrestling the unwieldy bales into neat stacks. Visions of the treasures my $5.00 would buy fueled my enthusiasm. My hay hooks were really flying—for about an hour. Then it seemed that each bale I bucked was 10 pounds heavier and six inches wider than the last one. My surging energy and enthusiasm soon diminished to a trickle.

When I stopped for lunch, my arms and back felt like rubber, and my forearms were stinging from scratches. By 3 P.M. I wasn't even half done with the job, but I was beat. I had told the farmer I would do the job in one day, and he was counting on me to finish. And I really wanted the money. But my fanciful visions of prosperity had long since evaporated in the summer heat. At five o'clock I went home, rationalizing that I could finish the job the next day.

In the morning, my once-eager commitment to the farmer was obliterated by my aching muscles and wounded pride. I phoned him with the lame excuse that I was sick and unable to finish the job. He was disappointed in me for reneging on my commitment, but at that moment I didn't care. He paid me $2.50 for my work and never hired me again.

A couple of summers later I got a job in a cherry orchard. It was a good job because I didn't have to pick the cherries, which is an awful way to earn spending money. Instead, I loaded the filled cherry bins into the farmer's immaculately preserved old truck and drove the bins to the brinery in town. The pay was good, and cruising around Salem in that classic truck was "cool."

On Friday of my first week, the farmer told me that he expected me to work on Saturday. I objected because I had a weekend fishing trip planned with my friends, a highlight of my summer. The farmer offered me a simple ultimatum: Work on Saturday or don't work at all. Again, my commitment to my employer floundered in the strong tide of my selfish pleasures. I quit my promising job to enjoy one brief weekend of fishing. Not only did I lose a great job, but also I ended up with a lousy job for the rest of the summer: picking fruit.

COMMITTED TO COMMITMENTS

There seem to be two prominent streams of thought today concerning commitments in the workplace. One stream winds warily away from commitments. "Don't commit yourself if you don't have to," it warns. "If you stay away from firm commitments, you can never disappoint your boss or your coworkers. And if you aren't committed, you can't be blamed for anything that goes wrong."

The second stream, illustrated by my early work experiences above, rushes swiftly and recklessly into commitments by assuring, "No problem, I can do it." But when easily committed people realize that the commitment isn't as simple to fulfill as they thought, the sidestepping and backpedaling begins. They look for an easy way out. They sometimes throw darts of blame at others, try to cover up their failures, or simply walk away as if they had never said yes in the first place.

Somewhere in the fertile ground between these two brackish streams of thought should be the working Christian. The Christian employee and employer in the workplace must be wholeheartedly committed to commitments. Unlike the fearful, apathetic, or lazy noncommitters, the Christian courageously, responsibly, and thoughtfully commits to work tasks. And unlike the mouth-in-gear-but-resolve-in-neutral easy committer, the Christian worker fulfills those commitments as thoroughly as possible.

A winsome witness on the job is someone who responsibly *makes* and faithfully *keeps* commitments. A commitment made but not kept on the job is at best a disappointment and at worst a lie to your coworkers. Solomon wisely warned, "It is better not to vow than to make a vow and not fulfill it" (Eccles. 5:5). He was speaking primarily of vows made to God. But the warning loses little punch when applied to commitments we make to superiors, peers, and subordinates in the office, factory, or store.

In the wide world of work, commitments make things go. Commitments move products and services from dreams to drawing boards. Commitments bring the pieces and parts together in production. Without commitments, your sales department couldn't move one unit of goods. Without commitments, your clients wouldn't think of identifying with your firm. As a Christian, your reputation for responsible commitment will serve as a major plank in your platform of ministry to your coworkers.

Targets for Your Commitments

As a teenage employee, I had about as much strength of commitment as a jellyfish has backbone. But as I finished school and moved into my career, my understanding of the importance of commitment matured. After a year as a technician in Lockheed's missile and space division and several months in the air force's electronics school, I joined Tektronix in 1966. During my 23 years at Tek, I faced obstacles much greater than hay bales in the summer sun. But I stayed on the job. I was tempted by diversions infinitely more rewarding than lazy fishing trips along the Santiam River. But I kept working. The circle of my commitments ballooned from two disgruntled farmers to more than 600 people under my employ in 1987. But I stayed committed to my career until God said it was time to move on.

Nothing has been more instrumental to my success as a Christian in the business world than learning how to make and keep commitments. There are three critical levels of commitment that will make or break your credibility as a Christian where you work.

Make a commitment to Christ. I opened my life to the Lordship of Jesus Christ as a youth in Salem, Oreg. But like so many believers, I found it easy to compartmentalize my faith. I was quite angelic at church, on youth outings, and at Christian camps. But when I moved into the nonchurch environment of school and unbelieving friends—which occupied the majority of my time—I changed colors. Like the chameleon, my appearance was dictated by my surroundings. Inside the Christian circle I wanted to look like a Christian. But outside that circle I wasn't always sure. It took awhile for me to see that true commitment to Christ must transcend the tidy borders of the church calendar and encompass my total schedule, my total life.

As working Christians, most of us spend a significant amount of our time and energy in the non-Christian workplace. We are easily swept up in the less-than-heavenly pursuits of secular companies and worldly coworkers. When we step up to the time clock to punch in for our shift, we are tempted at the same time to punch out as Christians.

Christians must make a conscious commitment to be God's people in the office, store, or factory as much as in the sanctuary. The church is merely the classroom for our faith. The outside world—especially the secular workplace—is the lab where we apply our faith. You don't pass the course of Christian commitment unless you do the lab work in the world.

One of the primary ways to apply your commitment to

Christ on the job is through prayer. While working at Tek, my daily 40-minute commute to the office afforded me time to pray for the tasks, decisions, and problems I would face that day. I used my time walking between offices to pray for the people I worked with. I consciously imagined Jesus moving through the office and labs of our campus, exercising His Lordship over people, projects, and problems.

During one project, two of my staff members were constantly at each other's throats in bitter disagreement. Both had told me independently that they would rather quit than work with the other. So I reserved a conference room and scheduled a meeting for the three of us. I wanted to clear the air and make peace between them, even though I feared that I might lose them both.

As I often do when facing a meeting to resolve a conflict, I arrived at the conference room five minutes early for prayer. I praised God for His Lordship over my life, my responsibilities, and my staff. I prayed that the room would be filled with the power of Christ to bring peace and understanding to my coworkers.

When the three of us sat down together, it was as if Jesus himself was chairing the meeting. I didn't say more than 10 words, but somehow peace and openness took over, and my two staff members resolved their differences in about 15 minutes. The scene has been repeated many times as I have attempted to establish the Lordship of Christ over every facet of my work through prayer.

Living out your commitment to Christ at work involves more than prayer. It involves the application of love, righteousness, integrity, and justice in every one of your responsibilities and relationships on the job. Subsequent chapters will illustrate the practical expression of these qualities in the work environment.

Make a commitment to your company. I had been working at Tektronix about 14 years when I was appointed to start up and manage the production of a new computer system for software development. Our organization did very well for the first 2 years, but we couldn't get the new products out fast enough to keep up with the demand. As we lagged behind, our competition caught up and passed us.

One day, our group vice president walked in and said, "Jerry, the senior exec wants you out. You've got to find another job."

I couldn't believe it. I'd been fired. My team had played hard and well, but we hadn't been fast enough to grab and hold a strong market position. As it sometimes happens in professional sports, my boss had to fire me and bring in another "coach" to rekindle a winning tradition.

But I had made a commitment to Tektronix and its values. God had placed me there, and I didn't want to leave until He called me elsewhere. At the time Tektronix was employing about 20,000 people, a huge corporation, so there were plenty of jobs within the company for which I could apply. But it was difficult to find another position that was comparable in responsibility to the one I had left. Even though I had received several promising offers outside the company, I opted for a demotion in order to stay at Tek. I stepped down the ladder and submitted to a lengthy pay freeze.

My new working environment was more difficult, and the management style of my new boss was uncomfortably different. But I was determined to live out my commitment to Tektronix until God directed me elsewhere. And I'm glad I stayed. Over the next eight years I rose through the ranks of the company and received many rewards as a manager. And I was able to share my testimony for Christ with literally hundreds of coworkers in my mission field.

Have you ever paused to consider that your present job is part of God's will for your life? He put you there. He has a plan for you there. He wants to use you there as His instrument of blessing and ministry. Maybe you're not being paid what you're worth. Maybe your boss is a tyrant, or your coworkers are goldbricks. Maybe your company's competitors are running circles around you. It doesn't matter. You applied for the job, they offered you the job, and you accepted the job. In bad times or good, you need to live out your commitment as a loyal employee until God directs you elsewhere.

Make a commitment to follow through. On one project I managed, I needed to hire a manufacturing manager for our organization. The man I selected—I'll call him Ted—was eager to take the position. Because our organization was small and the project was of such a critical nature, I asked Ted to commit himself to me, the project, and the team for a minimum of one year. Ted did so willingly.

But after seven months on the job, Ted announced that he was leaving to take a better position with a rival company. His departure was a major blow that negatively affected the success of our project and the large number of people working on it. "Ted, you made a commitment to the group," I challenged. "How can you leave us and the project at such a critical time?"

His reply epitomizes the position of the easy committer who abandons his resolve for greener pastures: "How could I turn down such a great opportunity?"

Following through on your commitments is important. Without follow-through, people are let down, projects are crippled, and your credibility as a team player is impaired. Each of your commitments to your boss, fellow workers, and employees is even more important than your commitment to your company and its goals or values. When you make and keep a commitment to someone, you place value on that individual. The relationship between coworkers who value one another through faithful commitments grows strong and productive. You may fail in a commitment to a product, but resolve to succeed in your commitment to relationships. Even when the product commitments are in danger, resolve to cherish and nourish your coworkers by faithfully fulfilling your personal commitments to them.

Once I was part of a team at Tektronix that made extraordinary commitments to do things we didn't know how to do. We gave it our best shot and still failed at the project.

But our team came out of the experience stronger than we went in because we purposely valued each other's priorities in the losing effort. As Christian workers, we labor alongside people whom God loves and for whom Christ died. We must similarly love and affirm our coworkers by being faithful in our commitments to them.

Counterfeit Commitments in Circulation

Underneath the large, inclusive canopy of commitments to Christ, company, and coworkers dwells an endless number of day-to-day, moment-to-moment, project-to-project commitments. Do any of the following statements of commitment sound familiar?

- I'll review your proposal before tomorrow's meeting.
- We'll make a personal call on each account every quarter.
- The setup and printing will cost no more than $89.50.
- I'll have the frozen food case scrubbed out by five o'clock.
- I can make the repairs and have it back to you by Tuesday.
- You can schedule your vacation anytime after May 1.
- I'll order it today, and you can pick it up Friday.
- Let me put you on hold for one minute.
- Your appointment is for 3 P.M. sharp.
- We always give a Christmas bonus.

What would the work atmosphere at your shop or office be like if every commitment like these were kept faithfully? You would probably think that heaven couldn't be much better! Realistically, of course, daily commitments in the workplace are made and broken every day. One reason for this failure is that some of them are counterfeit commitments being passed off as the real thing. Be sure that the commitments you make to your fellow workers are the genuine article, not one of the following counterproductive counterfeits.

An intended commitment. Sometimes we are guilty of saying something like, "I'll have the preliminary design ready by Tuesday," when we really mean, "I'll *try* to have the preliminary design ready by Tuesday." An intended commitment is a "maybe" camouflaged as a "can do." When you circulate intended commitments, you build false hopes and expectations in your coworkers and customers. You set them up for a fall, and people have little trust or respect for someone who keeps knocking them down. Solomon described the intended committer poetically when he wrote: "Like clouds and wind without rain is a man who boasts of gifts he does not give" (Prov. 25:14).

A false commitment. I worked on a computer system for a manager who promised the corporate execs that he would have the project in on time. But Eric knew, as we all did, that the project was hopelessly behind schedule. He had made the initial commitment without counting the cost. As we got into it, Eric realized that he didn't have the schedule or the resources to come in on time. He wanted to meet his commitment, and he kept assuring the execs that he would make it. But we didn't make it.

When the higher-ups discovered that Eric never had the resources to meet the schedule, they were furious. Eric rationalized his way out of his commitment by citing the real reasons why we didn't hit the target. But his persistent false commitment almost to the last minute earned him a landslide vote of nonconfidence from superiors and subordinates alike.

False commitment is quick to promise, "I'll do it," while holding in reserve a pack of excuses in case of failure: "It took too much time"; "It got too big"; "It got too complicated"; "My resources played out."

Why do workers—even some Christian workers—resort to intended commitments and false commitments instead of stating and sticking by the real thing? In some cases, these counterfeit commitments reflect a sincere desire for accomplishment. It's a good idea, and we know it needs to be done, so we make a rash promise. Furthermore, spurious commitments are often made to get people off our backs, to please the boss or the staff, to buy time, or to cover up our inability to produce. Yet, these half-truths only serve to create false expectations and foster distrust—both of which are counterproductive to the Christian's witness in the work environment.

Guidelines for Productive Commitments

The value of making and keeping commitments at all costs is underscored by King David in Psalm 15. He begins the psalm by asking the rhetorical question, "Lord, who may dwell in your sanctuary? Who may live on your holy hill?" (v. 1). Then David itemizes the premium qualities that he knew God was looking for in godly men and women, such as blamelessness, righteousness, truthfulness, justice, and purity of speech. Included in the list is the person "who keeps his oath even when it hurts" (v. 4). God is looking for Christians on the job who will commit themselves to their commitments "even when it hurts." Here are some practical ways by which our response to this criterion can be activated on the job:

Be decisive. Find out exactly what your boss, coworkers, or subordinates want you to do. Ask them to be specific, perhaps putting their request in writing. Then respond with a clear yes, no, or "I have a better idea"—also in writing if possible. Without a clear, certain response, your team may read in a yes when you mean maybe or no.

And be courageous enough to say no when you cannot meet the commitment. An up-front no will save you from the hassles and hurt of a hope-so yes that must be aborted midstream. Solomon's wisdom on the subject is pithy and picturesque: "An honest answer is like a kiss on the lips" (Prov. 24:26).

Clarify your commitments. State clearly what you *are* committing and what you *are not* committing to. Equivocal responses give rise to unrealistic expectations and set the stage for disappointment, hurt, and anger.

Floyd heard that I had a new position open on our

team for which I was interviewing candidates. The new role would be a step up for Floyd, so he persistently hounded me for the promotion. "You probably have the qualifications, Floyd," I responded, trying to fend off his constant badgering. "And I think you could do the job." I was trying to offer Floyd some hope without locking myself into a commitment to him.

But my unclear response backfired on me. As it turned out, Floyd was not the most qualified among the candidates, so I gave the job to someone else. Floyd was incensed because he thought he had extracted a commitment from me to hire him. I was wrong to give Floyd unfounded hope. I should have clearly told him during the interview, "I cannot promise you the job, Floyd. But I will evaluate your qualifications along with the other candidates and let you know what I decide."

Qualify your commitments. Some of our commitments at work must be made in the face of possible risks and obstacles to their completion. If you make a decisive commitment to one of these chancy tasks, be sure to qualify your commitment honestly, based on the information you have. Itemize the obstacles that need to be overcome in order for you to fulfill the commitment.

For example, your boss at the supermarket asks, "Can you fill the self-serve hosiery rack from back stock before you leave today?" Ordinarily, making such a commitment would be no problem. But the store is running a big canned food sale, and you may be needed at the cash register. So your qualified response to your boss may be, "I will fill the rack provided I can get free from the check stand. If you allow me at least two hours on the floor, I am sure I can finish the task."

Solomon wrote, "It is a trap for a man to dedicate something rashly and only later to consider his vows" (Prov. 20:25). Jesus urged His disciples to count the cost before making a commitment (Luke 14:28-33). When stating a conditional commitment, a realistic estimate will produce realistic expectations.

Give commitments priority. If the project is a high-value item to you, you will automatically make it a high priority. But if you perceive the difficulty of a project to be greater than its value to you, it will be a low priority for you. Remember, however, that the project is high value to someone, and you made a commitment to that person. At that point, that which is a priority to someone else *must* become a priority to you, whether you feel like making it so or not.

Communicate during the task. Once you have made a commitment, especially if it is conditional upon certain obstacles that need to be overcome, keep people informed about your progress. Let them know when you're on schedule or in danger of falling behind. Write frequent, informative memos. Visit often with the principal players in the conference room and at the coffee machine. Keep a no-surprises profile, and you will likely garner a no-surprises response.

When you fail, admit it. You promised you would have the filing completed by Friday night, but you blew it. You assured that you would come in under bid, but you wrinkled the company's bottom line on the project. Don't make excuses. Don't place blame. Don't try to cover yourself. Admit your failure and apologize. Take your lumps and your medicine. Learn from your mistake and go on.

I was nearing the end of my first three years at Tek, and I was anxious to move into a new and more challenging position. I knew I was capable of moving up, and I had been asking God to open the doors to a promotion. But for months I couldn't so much as interest a manager in looking at my résumé.

One morning, I was so desperate that I searched out a deserted lab where I could pray. The lab was used for visual testing of display instruments, so it was almost as dark as midnight inside. I sat alone in the darkness, pouring out my complaint to God.

Suddenly, the voice of God, as close to audible as I've

ever heard it, thundered a crystal-clear response into my heart: "Until you learn to love what I have already given you to do, I will not give you something else." God wasn't impressed with my potential for upward mobility. He was calling me to make a day-to-day commitment to a day-to-day job.

I was so stunned by the truth of God's word to my heart that my emotions cracked and broke. "I will love my job, and I will do it faithfully," I surrendered, weeping. Then I told God that I would commit myself to my present job even if it meant that I never received a promotion at Tek.

That afternoon, I received a phone call from a manager who wanted to interview me for a new position. I got the job.

You may be anticipating a successful career of 20 or 30 years or more. But God will only dispense it to you in fragile one-day sections. Allow your commitment to focus on the tasks of the day, and let Him take care of your tomorrows.

· 2 ·

Try Hard to Be Number Two

MARGE WAS A TALENTED, capable woman who worked for me for a brief time. She was one of the most aggressive and confrontive employees I've ever known. She craved responsibility, achievement, and authority, and she was driven to scale the company ladder as rapidly as possible. Marge tracked awards and promotions like a hungry lioness stalks a wounded gazelle.

On the positive side, Marge was really into her work and always ready to try new challenges. But, unfortunately, the negatives of her drive and ambition outweighed the positives. Marge was so locked into advancement that her coworkers and superiors became nothing more than stepping-stones to her personal career goals. She used everything and everyone to serve her ends. She wanted complete freedom in her areas of responsibility and demanded unquestioned allegiance to her decisions.

Despite her exceptional ability, Marge was known only as an incorrigible tyrant to her managers and peers. She ran roughshod over the ideas and opinions of others. Nobody wanted to work with her, and many of her fellow workers came to me asking to be reassigned—away from her department.

Robert, another employee of mine, was extremely bright. He was a self-appointed authority on every subject in the office, even in areas where he had no responsibility. He continually talked down to peers and subordinates alike. He let everybody know that their ideas were inferior in light of his intellect and insight.

When I confronted Robert on his offensive attitude and actions, he responded arrogantly, "I don't have a problem; they have a problem. I'm more intelligent than anyone on the team, including you, Jerry." Then when I told him that I was demoting him for his disruptiveness and ineffectiveness, Robert retorted, "You can't do that." In spite of his self-proclaimed superiority, Robert was forced to learn something new about his boss and his job that day!

"I'VE GOTTA BE ME"

Marge and Robert illustrate an all-too-common attitude that pervades our places of employment today. This attitude and its corresponding actions are usually expressed more subtly than the two blatant examples above. But this mentality is so widespread in the secular work community that Christian employees can easily and quite unconsciously become swept up in it.

In the kindest terms, this attitude can be identified as "the quest for independence." But beneath this noble-sounding pursuit lurks a self-centered, self-seeking drive that demands rights, recognition, and free rein. Perhaps this attitude was best characterized in the business world by the power lunches and assertiveness seminars that became popular in the mid-1980s.

Assertiveness—that's the attitude we're talking about. If the impulses and urges of this egotistical drive could be translated into plain English, here's what they would sound like:

• Toot your own horn; do your own thing; command your own destiny. You have your rights in this company. Stand up for them, and oppose anyone who violates them.

• Be bold and tough; don't back down to anyone. If you show weakness, your coworkers will disrespect you and take advantage of you.

• Be aggressive or you'll never get anything. Seize every opportunity and grab everything you want.

- Don't depend on anyone; don't trust anyone. Your coworkers are only out to achieve their own ends.

- Strive for power and influence over your peers. It's the only way to get what you want.

Wise King Solomon wrote some strong words about the overly assertive individual, labeling him a fool: "A fool finds no pleasure in understanding but delights in airing his own opinion" (Prov. 18:2). As we shall see later in this chapter, the attitude of self-assertiveness is generally at cross-purposes with the biblical attitude God desires to nurture in the Christian employee. But first, let's identify several of the destructive facets of the "I've gotta be me" syndrome.

"I've Gotta Be Free"

Assertive people crave freedom. They want to say what they want to say when they want to say it and do what they want to do when they want to do it. They tolerate few checks or balances. They are poor at following directions because they must be free to do things their way.

Assertive people dominate others. In their frantic hunger for their own space, they gobble up the space of their coworkers. They shut down everyone who infringes on their territory. They are experts at put-downs, and they excel in one-way communication—speaking but not listening. Their own ideas and purposes are so consumptive that other good ideas and pertinent issues are overlooked.

Art came to work with a master's degree in business administration from Harvard University. Nobody else in Art's work group had an MBA, and it was soon apparent that Art's degree was his cherished passport to personal career freedom.

Whenever ideas were exchanged in a planning meeting, Art would immediately critique them and the employees who offered them. He confidently asserted that his education gave him a superior perspective. Consequently, he could not and would not receive ideas from others. Art became a little autocrat, championing his own causes while stomping the life out of everybody else's ideas.

Art's coworkers were understandably annoyed by his insensitivity. I sat down with him one day and said, "Art, do you realize that most of the people on your team would just as soon shoot you as look at you? You are foisting your own ideas with no regard for the ideas of your team members." Characteristic of assertive freedom-seekers, Art was unaware of the contempt, frustration, and anger his actions spawned in his peers.

One seminar instructor I heard called this syndrome the "tyranny of freedom." When you brashly claim your office or department as your sole domain, you tend to tyrannize as serfs the poor souls who must work with you there. The feelings and contributions of others are ignored. Many positive ideas and relevant issues are obliterated. And the atmosphere surrounding the affected relationships is poisoned with bitterness and resentment.

"I've Gotta Be Right"

Another aspect of the harmful assertive attitude on the job is the consuming need to be right. We're not talking here about selecting right and good over wrong and evil. Such a discipline is intrinsic to the pursuit of maturity at every level of Christian experience. Rather, we're talking about the neurotic, prideful insistence that our solutions are always the right solutions and our ideas are always the best ideas.

The person who needs to be right is so possessed by the value of his own idea that he cannot see the value of other ideas. Indeed, when you spend all your energy advancing your own position, you are unable to tolerate other positions. You cannot see them as viable alternatives, only as rivals that must be discredited and disarmed.

Once I was putting together a sales program with about five other coworkers. I had a brilliant idea for the campaign, and I proudly announced it to the team. It was the right idea for what we wanted to do; I knew it, and I was locked into it. But my coworkers spent the rest of the meeting picking my idea apart. The more they criticized, the angrier I became. You dummies! I thought. Can't you see a good idea when it's right under your noses?

A few days later, I was talking with one of the members of that group, still insisting that my idea was right. "You may have been right, Jerry," he agreed, "but you were not seeking what was best." He told me that the "criticism" I perceived in the other group members was really their attempt to bring out some new ideas to complement my plan. In my possessive rush to be right, I had wrongly viewed their comments as affronts to my "perfect" idea. *I* was the dummy—an unwitting example of Solomon's proverb: "He who hates correction is stupid" (Prov. 12:1).

Pride is the motivator behind the bondage of having to be right. Somehow, we see our rightness connected to our worth as persons and employees. Pride cements us into place and prohibits our mobility toward other ideas or methods that may be as right as our own. Furthermore, our proud tenacity reaps other negative rewards. We lose credibility with others. We lose the confidence of others. Solomon said, "When pride comes, then comes disgrace" (Prov. 11:2). And our unyielding possessiveness reveals a lack of self-respect: "He who ignores discipline despises himself" (15:32).

"I've Gotta Win"

The need to be right is closely aligned with the need to win in day-to-day work activities. Job problems and opportunities are seen as contests in which the person with the best plan wins while all others lose. Winning is seen as the cherished pathway to favor with the upper echelons, to promotions, and to pay raises. Losing is shunned as certain doom for advancement. "Fight to be right; win at all costs," is the cry.

Once I presented an idea during a staff meeting, and everybody laughed. "That's a dumb idea," they chided. I was deeply humiliated and infuriated all at once. The other staff members had ganged up on the other end of the rope and dragged me through the mud. I was a loser. I was so deafened by my loss that I couldn't receive their ideas. I blocked out the rest of the meeting and refused to participate. And it serves them right, I reasoned to myself. They didn't hear my ideas.

If the "gotta win" individual can't be the big winner in a work situation, he must scramble to avoid being the big loser. I've been in many staff meetings where each member stated and defended a position or problem solution. Then, as the proponents jockeyed their ideas for supremacy, each began shooting down opposing ideas in order to keep their ideas aloft: "I don't see how that could work"; "It's bound to be expensive"; "This looks real tough, and your people couldn't pull it off last time"; "Your group hasn't met its quality objectives yet." It's like a childish game of king of the hill: You must knock everyone else down to stay on top.

Nobody likes to lose, because losing hurts. To the "gotta win" worker, there definitely is a thrill of victory and an agony of defeat—and a crushing agony of repeated defeat. Operating in a win-or-lose work environment can be a stressful, manic-depressive roller coaster ride.

Going Underground

What happens when the assertive person is not free to do what he wants, when he is not right, or when he doesn't win in the push and pull of work relationships? A common negative response is to go underground. Overtly, they yield to their superiors or defer to the winners. Superficially, they comply with the regulations that cramp their style or crimp their freedom. But covertly they rebel and resist. Their support is halfhearted at best. They subtly withhold some of their contributions from the process. The result is an insidious, destructive undermining of the organization.

Several years ago, I was working with two teams of engineers on a certain project. In order to complete the task, we needed to commit to a single microprocessor. One team insisted that we get a Motorola chip, and the other team was biased in favor of an Intel unit. After an energetic debate between the two teams, a selection was made. The team of engineers that "won" charged excitedly into the project, enthusiastic about working with the new "toy." But the losing team went underground. They participated, but they kept coming up with problems. They couldn't get the microprocessor to perform for them. "What a piece of junk," they grumbled.

As the project continued, the subversive, critical resistance of the losing team spread like a dark cloud over the entire group. The success of the project was in jeopardy. Finally, we had to pull the entire losing team off the project and replace them with a new team of engineers.

Passive, underground resistance in a work environment is like a cancer growing in an internal organ. On the surface, everything looks healthy. But inside, the life of the body is slowly being eaten away. As with a cancer, sometimes the only way to rid an organization of a destructive passive resistance is to excise it.

THE DISCIPLINE OF DEFERENCE

The antidote to the assertive, "gotta be free, gotta be right, gotta win" mentality in your work environment is deference. To defer means to yield with courtesy to the valid wishes or judgments of another. Instead of frantically fighting to be free, to be right, or to be the winner, we must learn to let go, step down, and step back. Instead of doggedly pushing for our rights, we must learn to humbly accept and faithfully fulfill our responsibilities—and leave the rest to God.

REMEMBER: People are more important than programs, projects, and products. People are eternal; the other stuff is only temporal. When we defer, we do so to honor our work relationships—bosses, coworkers, employees, customers. When we defer, we do so to cherish and nourish people for whom Christ died and to whom we owe the loving witness of genuine humility.

Let Go and Let God

Does deference mean we lie down and let people use us

for doormats? Are we supposed to abdicate our intellect and creativity and become spineless yes-persons to everyone on the job? Of course not! Deference doesn't mean *giving up*— forfeiting my role, responsibility, and resolve as an employee. Deference means *letting go*—yielding my cherished right to be free, to be right, and to win—and *letting God* determine the scope of my responsibility where I work.

Deference in our work relationships is an obedient response to the directive in James 4:10: "Humble yourselves before the Lord, and he will lift you up." In reality, our deference is primarily directed to God, our ultimate Employer. We are saying, "God, I defer to You as the Lord over my job, my boss, and my company. I resign as the self-imposed authority, and I let go of my selfish need for recognition, freedom, power, and position. I am content to let You place me and use me for Your glory where I work."

When you allow God to rightfully occupy the position of Chief Executive Officer where you work, you don't need to protect your freedom or your space. The CEO knows where you are and what you can handle. He will grant you grace and wisdom to occupy the territory you're assigned— great or small. You don't need to fight to be right or struggle to win. The CEO knows best how to use your skills to serve those around you. He's not looking for fighters or winners; He's looking for humble participants. He's not looking for ability in working Christians; He's looking for availability.

Notice the positive qualities that attend the Christian worker who allows God to superintend him: "He who heeds discipline shows the way to life" (Prov. 10:17); "Whoever heeds correction is honored" (13:18); "With humility comes wisdom" (11:2); "Whoever loves discipline loves knowledge" (12:1); "Whoever heeds correction gains understanding" (15:32).

Only when we let go of our "have it my way" attitude do we allow God the opportunity to do things His way in our work. Only when we let go of our "get what's coming to me" attitude can we give of ourselves responsibly in the work environment. Only when we release our death grip on our cherished opinions and judgments are we free to accept as valid the ideas of others. Only when we discharge the exaggerated estimation of our own importance can we accept and properly value those who work with us.

Step Down

A major key to exercising deference in our working relationships is acknowledging who the boss is. Most of us work for someone else—a manager, foreman, supervisor, director, leader, president, principal, etc. Even if you have ascended the infrastructural ladder several rungs, you still report to someone above you. He is the chief, and you are one of the braves. Theoretically, when the chief says, "Jump," you say, "How high?" on the way up.

But sometimes we don't want to jump. We disagree with the boss. Her ideas are off the wall. His solutions are wrong. We're tired of being pushed around by someone who doesn't know as much about our job as we do. Or we're just plain envious of someone who doesn't log in as many hours or sweat as much blood, but enjoys a plusher office, a fatter paycheck, and a longer vacation. Subtly, sometimes subconsciously, we challenge the throne by resisting or ignoring our superiors.

As the old saying goes, the boss may not always be right, but he's always the boss. We Christian braves have a more substantial reference point for our relationships with those above us. The apostle Paul wrote: "Remind the people to be subject to rulers and authorities, to be obedient, to be ready to do whatever is good, to slander no one, to be peaceable and considerate, and to show true humility toward all men" (Titus 3:1-2). Deference in the pecking order of the work staff means letting the boss be the boss. And if the boss is the boss, you can't be the boss. You must emotionally step down from any secretly assumed position of rebellion or resistance and wholeheartedly support the person God has installed over you.

"But what if my boss is a slave driver or a weasel?" you ask. "How can I submit to someone I don't even respect?"

There are some exceptions we will consider in succeeding chapters, but consider the general rule the apostle Peter laid down for first-century employees: "Slaves, submit yourselves to your masters with all respect, not only to those who are good and considerate, but also to those who are harsh" (1 Pet. 2:18). Paul's words are equally insightful: "Slaves, obey your earthly masters in everything; and do it, not only when their eye is on you and to win their favor, but with sincerity of heart and reverence for the Lord" (Col. 3:22). Be advised: When you invite Jesus Christ to be the CEO in your place of employment, it is His job to shape up your boss. Step down from any unauthorized position you have assumed. Let go of any unauthorized responsibilities you are guarding. Let God help you support and encourage those in authority over you. And trust God to deal with your superiors justly in His good time.

Step Back

Another key to exercising deference among our fellow workers is learning to step back from our jealously guarded points of view. Sometimes we get so locked into our own position that we are unable to see other viable possibilities. We can't see the forest of options for the trees of our prejudged conclusions.

In one of the groups I managed, I saw the need for an organizational change. Working alone, I plotted the restructure on paper, moving people and assignments around like pawns on a chessboard. The plan I devised was a good one, and I anticipated announcing it to my staff.

One of my staff members knew of the forthcoming announcement and came to see me. "I don't think it's wise for you to waltz in and lay this big change on them, Jerry," he cautioned. "They're intelligent people. They have some good ideas for reorganization too. I suggest that you consult with them and solicit their ideas, then use the input to formulate your plan."

He was right. The organizational plan I had worked out was one-dimensional: my view. Yet the shift was to be multidimensional, affecting dozens of people. I needed to step back from my vantage point and take a wider view. I decided to change my tack for the presentation meeting I had already scheduled.

Instead of blowing into the meeting with a plan cast in concrete, I opened the session up to discussion of our objectives. I asked my staff to suggest possible ways we could better meet our goals. The end result was an organizational plan similar to the one I had drawn up, but with some nuances that reflected positive input from the group. And since the group had participated in giving birth to the plan, the group owned the plan.

When you defer to your superiors, coworkers, or subordinates by stepping back from a defended position, several good things happen. First, your perspective changes. If you were sitting behind home plate at a baseball game for a couple of innings, then moved to a bleacher seat in the outfield, you would get a different view of the game. The players who were mere blurs on the outfield grass would become distinct. Your appreciation of the game would increase simply because you moved to a new location.

Similarly, when you purposely move back from a jealously guarded position by objectively questioning your goals or ideas or by allowing others to put your idea through the ringer, you have a better perspective of the entire issue.

Second, when you step back from your position and circulate to positions favored by your coworkers, you see the value of other positions. You may discover that your brilliantly unique solution is only one of several good solutions, and perhaps it's not even the best one. But you cannot gain the perspective of other seats in the ballpark until you get out of your own seat and move around.

Third, when you step back from your well-guarded position, you allow other people to move in and watch the ball game from your seat. It's the only way they can see the issue from your point of view. And if you don't back off, they will have a difficult time understanding and accepting your idea.

When you are possessive and defensive, you and your idea are about as inviting as a cold, dark castle with the drawbridge up and the moat full of alligators. The sign at the property line reads: "Private property. Keep out!" Your possessive grasping drives your coworkers away.

Instead, why not let go, open up, and invite your coworkers in? Release your idea to their inspection as you would open your home to invited guests. Welcome their insightful suggestions and criticisms. Allow them the privilege of participating in your project. You and your project will be the better for it—and so will your coworkers.

· 3 ·

Leave the Status Quo Behind

MY MOTHER BEGAN her childhood dirt poor in Arkansas. But during the late 1920s, an outbreak of malaria in the Ozarks forced her parents to pack the family's few belongings into a horse-drawn covered wagon and journey to Oklahoma. There the wagon and team were traded for a 1925 Model-T Ford truck. The floorboards from the wagon were fitted to make a new bed for the truck, and on they traveled to Texas. My grandfather got a job in an oil field near Odessa and earned enough money to move his family to Oregon. It was there that Mom met and married Dad in 1941.

Dad established himself as an electrician and earned a decent living. But the specter of poverty that haunted Mom through childhood prodded her to work also. For an unskilled housewife in rural Oregon, work meant picking fruit and vegetables. So from the time I was five years old, I worked in the harvest fields alongside my mother. We followed the crops through the spring, summer, and fall, picking daffodils, strawberries, cherries, peaches, pears, prunes, apples, gooseberries, hops, green beans, and cucumbers.

During one summer, Mom, my younger sister, Barbara, and I lived in a transient labor camp outside of Salem and worked the fields. It was hard work, but it was good work. I learned from my mother—rather reluctantly at times—the value and reward of manual labor.

At the same time, Dad personified for me the old adage,

"Any job worth doing is worth doing well." With Mom in the fields, I learned to work hard and long. And with Dad in his shop, I learned to do a job right. Even to this day, Dad would rather not start a job until he has the proper materials and tools to do it right. My parents' example of diligence and quality of effort has provided a solid foundation for my personal work ethic.

WHAT HAPPENED TO THE WORK ETHIC?

"It's so hard to find good help these days," we often joke with our coworkers. But sometimes it's not so funny. It really *is* hard to find good help these days. The tough, tireless work ethic that characterized our postdepression grandparents and post-World War II parents has become soft and lethargic. Unfortunately, our parents were driven by the fear of poverty to do too much for us. They were determined that their kids were not going to suffer as they did as children. So they handed everything to us on a silver platter and forgot to teach us the value of good, hard work.

Today, we live in an era clouded with the attitude of entitlement. The motto of past generations was, "Pull yourself up by your own bootstraps; work hard to get what you want." But much of today's work force marches under the banner that selfishly proclaims, "The world owes me a living, so give me what I have coming to me." The focus is no longer what we can do to serve the company, but what the company must do to serve us.

The faltering work ethic in America today can be characterized by several statements that reveal the "me-ism" of many employees. Perhaps you have heard these comments echoing through your place of employment. Perhaps you have uttered some of them yourself.

"It's Not My Job"

This worker is interested in fulfilling the basic requirements of his job description—and nothing more. He only does what is absolutely necessary to keep his job. He will not take initiative or responsibility beyond the borders of his work station. He clocks in at the stroke of starting time (or later if he can get away with it), performs the minimum daily requirements of his job, and clocks out at the stroke of quitting time (or earlier if he can get away with it).

This worker rarely sees the big picture of his company's product or service. He just does his small part, picks up his paycheck, and goes home.

"It's Not My Problem"

This worker refuses to take responsibility for the mistakes and failures of others. She comes on shift at the assembly line to discover that her predecessor forgot to install a couple of small wires. Instead of correcting the problem, she adds her six bolts to the faulty unit and sends it down the line. "It was his mistake, not mine," she rationalizes. "Besides, quality control will catch the error. That's their job."

These "faultless" employees are passive observers in the workplace. They will irresponsibly watch a coworker fail in a task without offering a word of warning or assistance.

"It's Not My Kind of Work"

This employee avoids any work that is trivial and mundane or that does not serve his self-centered goals. He is only interested in the tasks that will provide him high visibility, recognition, rewards, or promotions. He is purposely incompetent at any job he feels is beneath him, but he excels at those tasks that gain him the strokes or perks he craves.

"I've Always Done It This Way"

These workers won't try anything new or different for fear that it will upset the comfortable status quo. Often a group of fellow employees are committed to an unwritten pact not to rock the boat through innovation. After all, if one person works too fast or too hard, she may make the others look bad. If someone discovers a way to save time or steps in a task, somebody's job may be eliminated, or they may all lose their overtime. Mutual self-preservation is preferred over corporate improvement.

MOVING BEYOND THE STATUS QUO

For the Christian in the work environment, quality of effort is not just an admirable ethic from a previous generation. It is a relevant and biblically sound Christian value that must be cherished and practiced. Solomon advised, "Whatever your hand finds to do, do it with all your might" (Eccles. 9:10), and he warned, "One who is slack in his work is brother to one who destroys" (Prov. 18:9).

Furthermore, I believe the Christian's diligence on the job is a very practical response to Paul's command: "Offer your bodies as living sacrifices, holy and pleasing to God—this is your spiritual act of worship" (Rom. 12:1). We are to use our God-given physical strength and mental acumen to worship Him through the quality of our efforts on the job. And settling for the business-as-usual, don't-rock-the-boat status quo is an offering that is less than the potentially holy and pleasing sacrifice of wholehearted effort.

But if the status quo must go, how do we quantify and qualify our work? Of all that must be done at work, how much can we do? How much should we do? How can I know when I have fulfilled my Christian responsibilities at work? If I lean toward the perfectionistic side, I'll become a hopeless workaholic. If I lean the other way, I may rationalize myself out of work I should do. How good is "good enough" on my job?

We used a helpful phrase at Tek to define "good enough" for an instrument or project: fit for use. Even in our state-of-the-art engineering and production at Tek, we never did anything perfectly. It takes an interminable time to make something perfect. Engineers are sometimes so picky that they can overengineer a project in their attempts at perfection. So our goal was to assure that the finished product was fit for its intended use—that is, properly fitted to the level of expectation within given tolerances.

My dad, who is something of a perfectionist himself, has often said about something he was building, "It's got to be good enough for who and what it's for." As Christians, we must carefully evaluate the realistic expectations and needs of our superiors and coworkers, then be sure that our work is good enough for who and what it's for, adequately fitted for its intended use. Anything less is effort of questionable quality.

THE QUALITIES OF QUALITY WORK

Brad was an eager employee who wanted to advance. During a performance review, I rated his efforts at three on a scale of one to five, five being superior. Brad boldly asked what he must do to earn a level-four rating by his next review. So I gave him a written list of specific criteria for level-four production in his area. Brad left my office, list in hand, determined to meet the challenge and earn his level-four rating.

Brad was a tiger on the job for the next few months, and he accomplished every objective I had listed for him. But in the process, he virtually destroyed his relationships with his coworkers. He communicated to them brusquely through his actions, "Get out of my way; I don't have time for you. I'm too busy climbing to level four." He became so abrasive toward his group that nobody wanted to work with him. Though Brad's work production increased, his bull-in-a-china-shop approach to his peers ultimately proved to be counterproductive to our team.

During his next review, Brad proudly pointed to his accomplishments. "Brad, you performed quality work," I agreed. "But you affected the work environment so negatively through your uncooperative attitude that I'm dropping your rating to a two."

Brad was enraged. "But I completed the assignments you gave me," he protested hotly. "Relationships weren't on my list!" I reminded him that positive relationships are always an unwritten priority on everybody's list.

Quality is not just what we do, it's what we do plus how we do it. Quality is not just a product, it's the product plus the process of producing it. The quality of Brad's product was hollow because he littered the trail with the bleeding bodies of his coworkers in the process.

The following guidelines specify some practical steps you can take to assure that your work—both product and process—is of the quality that pleases everyone in your company, from your heavenly CEO on down.

Rise Above and Beyond the Call of Duty

When you commit to a job description, project role, or individual task, make it your goal to do more than is expected of you. Jesus said: "If someone forces you to go one mile, go with him two miles. Give to the one who asks you, and do not turn away from the one who wants to borrow from you" (Matt. 5:41-42). A Christian on the job should be ready to give more than is requested, serve more than is required, and do more than is expected—all with an attitude of love and helpfulness.

One of my fellow Christians at Tek was named Marvin. His first job was testing and calibrating electronic equipment. When the units arrived in the lab from assembly, Marvin and his coworkers turned them on. The units either worked or smoked! If they worked, they were calibrated to measurements in microseconds. If they smoked, Marvin's group troubleshot the components and corrected the problem, then calibrated them. Then the completed units went to quality assurance for the seal of approval.

Marvin and his fellow workers were allotted a standard amount of time to test each instrument. While most of the techs in the lab paced themselves to meet the standard time, Marvin competed with himself to beat it. He refused to be confined to the status quo. His goal was to see how many instruments he could test and calibrate each day while staying within the specifications of quality assurance. His productivity increased steadily until he was consistently doing twice the work that was expected of him in the time allowed.

Another technician in the lab was very fast, but he cut corners on his calibrations. He played the odds by eliminating some checks in order to push the units through. But he earned a bad reputation with the quality assurance department for his sloppy work. It's one thing to work fast and set production records. It's another thing to work fast without sacrificing the quality of your work.

As a result of Marvin's commitment to do more than expected in the calibration lab, he always received good performance reviews and salary increases. But the greatest result was the trust and respect he earned from his superiors, peers, and subordinates, which formed a solid platform for Marvin's ministry for Christ at Tek.

When Something Goes Wrong, Try to Fix It

Quality on the job requires that we take broad responsibility for what is right where we work. When something goes wrong in your area, make it right as soon as possible. When something goes wrong in someone else's area and you have the power to fix it, do so. Resist evasive excuses such as "I didn't break it, so I don't have to fix it"; "It's not my department, so I'm not responsible"; "It's somebody else's turn to be responsible."

We sometimes feel as if we are fixing the problem by merely spotting it and reporting it. For instance, your co-worker, Howard, forgot to turn off the store's outside lights when he came in this morning. The lights are Howard's job, so you take 10 minutes tracking him down to tell him he forgot the lights. But often it is more expedient simply to correct the problem. Turn the outside lights off yourself and save both you and Howard the extra steps.

Or let's say that you are walking down the hall and spy a used paper towel that has been carelessly thrown on the floor. You could phone the custodian and have him pick it up. You could mutter disgustedly about the slobs you work with as you walk past it. Or you could take responsibility for righting the wrong by picking it up and disposing of it properly. There are many times when you will consume less energy by solving the problem yourself than you would by stewing about it or trying to nail the person who may be responsible.

Once I heard about an employee of an overnight delivery service who modeled a responsible attitude for problems beyond his realm of responsibility. His truck broke down as he hurried to deliver a very important cargo on time. When he reported the breakdown to his office, the driver learned that no other trucks were available to help him meet his delivery deadline.

But instead of yielding to a seemingly insurmountable problem, the delivery man took personal responsibility for a solution. He chartered a helicopter with his own money in order to deliver the important parcel on time. His company lauded him as an exemplary employee.

"But," you may object, "how am I supposed to solve my own problems and get my own work done if I'm spending all my time solving other people's problems?" Certainly there are priorities you must observe. But remember: A commitment to quality is a commitment to do more than is expected. You must be ready to spend a little more time and effort on your coworkers in order to fulfill your quality commitment.

Do the Unimportant Job

A Christian employee's commitment to quality of effort means that he will gladly accept and cheerfully complete even the most menial, unimportant tasks. Anybody can volunteer for the high-visibility, important, fun jobs. But a strong element of the believer's witness on the job is his enthusiasm about accepting the low-visibility, dirty job that nobody else wants.

My friend Ed worked as a part-time clerk in a drugstore while attending Christian college. In the back of the drugstore was a room about eight feet square called the trash room. Throughout the day, the full-time clerks tossed their empty cartons and rubbish into the trash room. Each evening when Ed reported to work, the trash room was full with no room for the rubbish from the evening shift. Somebody had to climb into the trash room, break down the empty cartons, and flatten the trash to make room for the evening crew's deposits. It was a dirty job that everyone avoided.

At first, Ed rationalized himself out of the dreaded task. He was a clerk, not a custodian. He was part-time, temporary help, not a career clerk needing to impress the boss to advance. And he was a ministerial student, thinking himself somewhat above such domestic labor.

But Ed was also committed to serve Christ and live as a faithful witness before his fellow workers. He saw that volunteering to perform the nightly "trash room stomp" was one way to serve Christ and his coworkers at the drugstore. So Ed humbly and cheerfully accepted the trash room chore as a ministry to Christ. The silent testimony of Ed's commitment to his unpleasant task opened the door to numerous verbal testimonies to his coworkers.

I've known numerous managers in many companies who were so impressed with their positions that they wouldn't answer their own phones. I've watched them sit idly beside their ringing phones while their secretaries raced across the room to answer. "The phone is my secretary's job," I've heard them say. For the Christian worker, there should be no job too small or too menial, including cleaning up your own work area, picking up hastily thrown paper towels in the rest room, stomping the trash room, or answering phones.

And you don't need to wave a flag or make an announcement calling attention to your noble efforts. It's OK if nobody knows you tidied up the lunchroom or switched off a machine that was thoughtlessly left running. Your reward is the good feeling of knowing you did the right thing whether anyone else knows about it or not. We will discuss this attitude of self-sacrifice in greater detail in chapter 7.

Find a Better Way

A Christian committed to quality of effort should be a leader in finding better ways to do his job. We must press beyond the comfortable status quo and maintain a mentality of innovation. We should be continually asking ourselves, "How can I do my work faster and more efficiently? How can I save time, steps, materials, and money for myself, my department, and my company? How can I help eliminate errors, expedite production, increase sales, and minimize returns and redos?"

A local manufacturer used to inventory every single piece of electronic assembly hardware once a month. It meant that the warehouse spent many tedious man-hours each month counting piles of screws, clips, and wires that cost practically nothing. Ron understood the importance of inventorying expensive parts, but he felt that they were wasting time and money meticulously counting five-for-a-penny screws every month.

Ron suggested that they estimate the count of several components by bucket or binful instead of keeping a written record of each tiny item. When the warehousemen, for instance, saw that a bucket of screws was running low, they would simply order enough to fill the bucket. It was a simple idea, but it saved the company countless man-hours. And it happened because somebody was looking for a better way.

Many corporations over the years have sent their employees to a highly respected, quality training program in Florida. The program is an intensive seminar stressing principles for improving quality in job-related products, environment, and relationships.

One of the most helpful insights I gained from the program is that every worker has a primary customer in the work environment. Interestingly, your primary customer is usually not the person outside the company walls who buys your products or services. Your primary customer is the person your work goes to next. In an assembly line, your primary customer is the person who receives what you produce in order to add the next part. If you are a typist, it's the person who must sign and send the letter you type. If you're a cashier at a supermarket, it's the person who boxes the groceries you run across the scanner. If you're a fruit picker, it's the person who takes your boxes of fruit and loads them onto the truck for delivery.

The first step in developing quality relationships with your coworkers is learning to treat your primary customer right. Discover his needs, and go out of your way to meet them. Discover his problems, and work hard to solve them. Discover what you can do to make his job easier, more productive, or more enjoyable, and do it. Think of your primary customer as the one individual you must please in order for your job to succeed.

The Ford Motor Company has made some great strides in quality work relationships through their "quality is job one" campaign. Each worker on the assembly line spends some time at the next station downline observing what his coworker does with the product. Then each worker visits the next station upline to see how the product coming down the pike is prepared. On both sides workers are encouraged to state their needs and wishes and mutually commit themselves to comply. They have learned to treat each other right. The result has been a dramatic increase in the quality of each car that leaves the Ford plant.

An important second step in developing quality relationships is to acknowledge and affirm the efforts of your coworkers. Compliment others for their good work with a memo, card, or quick phone call. Celebrate the accomplishments of your coworkers with an occasional lunch out together. Recognize even the innovative attempts that end in failure by saying, "Nice try. Keep the good ideas coming." And liberally distribute among your coworkers the two most affirming words in the English language: "Thank you!"

Don't Just Stand There, Do Something

Warren was one of our best electrical design engineers at Tek. But he was never satisfied with his work environment. He was always seeking to improve his methods and engineering tools. He always completed his design work well and ahead of schedule. Then he would spot something else that needed to be done and find a way to help do it. Once he even learned how to write software in order to help the software engineers solve a problem. Warren found great satisfaction in looking for problems that needed to be solved and finding ways to solve them.

Some people, like Warren, are natural self-starters. They don't need much external motivation; they seem to be motivated from within. Initiators on the job make things happen and keep things moving.

I believe that all Christians are called to be initiators where they work, whether or not they are natural self-starters. We are not to be passive observers standing around waiting for someone else to act. We should lead the way in quality work by being initiators, facilitators, contributors, and participants. We would do well to remind ourselves daily as we arrive on the job, "I'm here to initiate actions of love and helpfulness to my superiors, peers, and coworkers. I'm here to do something, not to stand around."

Practically speaking, initiators arrive at work on time or ahead of time, look for work instead of waiting for work to find them, return phone calls promptly, offer assistance readily, tackle difficult problems head-on instead of skirting them, and willingly spend extra time and energy getting the job done on schedule.

Put the Lord's Signature on Your Work

Paul encouraged the Christian servants in Colossae, "Whatever you do, work at it with all your heart, as working for the Lord, not for men . . . It is the Lord Christ you are serving" (3:23-24). The most haunting feelings I experience as a worker dedicated to quality are from knowing I did not give the job my best effort. Conversely, my most gratifying feelings come from doing a thorough, quality job that I can proudly present to the Lord.

For the Christian worker, the Lord Jesus is the quality assurance supervisor. He must sign off on your work before it is acceptable. He knows what you are doing and how it should be done. You must complete your work tasks in such a way that you can imagine His signature of approval on them. Rest assured: When your work is good enough for Him, it will be good enough for anyone.

· 4 ·

Be Ready When Murphy Strikes

ALMOST EVERYBODY has heard of Murphy's Law. Briefly stated, Murphy's Law warns, "Anything that can go wrong will go wrong." Perhaps the classic example of this satirical axiom predicts that if you drop a slice of buttered toast, it will always land butter side down. We've all had fun blaming a fictional character named Murphy for the crazy little things that go wrong in our daily lives.

But when things go wrong in the world of our work experience, it's anything but a laughing matter. We're not talking about little goofs like toast falling on the floor. We're talking about production schedules that go unmet, business plans that fail, and coworkers who botch assignments or don't show up for work. We're talking about software glitches, machinery breakdowns, cost overruns, unfilled back orders, missized parts, budget shortfalls—and I'm sure you can add several problems to the list that are unique to your work environment and job description! Errors like these are not funny. They sometimes cost the company money, they often burden the staff with extra work, and they always tax our patience and test the mettle of relationships on the job.

Let's be honest: We live in an imperfect world, and we work with imperfect people—including ourselves. Things *will* go wrong at work. There's no getting around it. The challenge for the working Christian is knowing how to handle the problems when they hit. We must discover how

51

to honor Christ and our coworkers in an atmosphere where problems, imperfections, and unrealized expectations are the rule rather than the exception.

Don't Be a Knee-jerk Employee

One of the reasons problems on the job are problems for us is because they often take us by surprise. We expect machinery to run smoothly, we expect coworkers to show up on time and work efficiently, and we expect customers to fulfill or exceed our hopeful sales projections. We are often so idealistic—and sometimes so perfectionistic—in our work tasks that we allow interruptions, failures, or breakdowns to sneak up behind us. When the unwanted problem suddenly shouts, "Boo!" we generally react *against* it instead of respond *to* it. And knee-jerk reactions against work problems are usually counterproductive.

An Aggressive Explosion

There are two wrong ways in which workers react against problems on the job. The first is a visible, outward reaction—an emotional explosion by which we subconsciously disassociate ourselves from responsibility for the problem. An emotional outburst may serve to cover up ("It's not my fault!"), accuse ("It's his fault"), lash out ("If you think I'm at fault, you're crazy!"), or retaliate ("You're not going to get away with it!"). These overt, aggressive, and sometimes caustic reactions against problems remind me of the person described in Prov. 18:2: "A fool finds no pleasure in understanding but delights in airing his own opinions."

Duane was a young manager at Tek, managing his first project. During the course of the project, somebody on Duane's team let an assigned task fall through the cracks, delaying the project. When Duane heard about the problem, he blew up. "I don't know how any responsible person could make such a mistake!" he screamed at his team. Duane continued his blistering verbal tirade with abusive and degrading name-calling.

When the smoke cleared a few days later, Duane realized the foolishness of his outburst and apologized for his vitriolic reaction. But the emotional wound he had inflicted on his team refused to heal. Despite Duane's sincere apology, his team could not overlook his insensitive reaction to a relatively harmless snafu. A storm of animosity enveloped the team for the duration of the project.

Harley was an executive on my boss's staff who had risen rapidly through the ranks as a brilliant and creative designer/engineer. But Harley was like a stick of dynamite in problem situations, and anyone who confronted him with a problem in staff meeting became his lighted fuse. Even the slightest criticism of Harley's actions or projects set off an explosive reaction. When crossed, Harley could unleash the most abusive, attacking, and humiliating verbal assault I've ever heard.

As a result, nobody wanted to work with Harley. Furthermore, his coworkers avoided many topics that needed to be discussed in staff meeting simply because nobody wanted to set Harley off. Sadly, Harley's violent, irrational reaction against problems destroyed his work relationships and led to his termination.

A Passive Retreat

An opposite but equally nonproductive reaction against work problems is passive retreat from involvement. Like frightened rabbits in a forest full of hunters, passive retreaters hear the gunshots of problems and scamper for the nearest hollow log. Their reaction against problems is to fade into the woodwork through noninvolvement. Their creed is to say little or nothing, avoid confrontation, keep the emotional waters from getting stirred up, and refuse to get involved in hammering out a solution—even when they know a solution!

Vicente, another very creative member of my boss's staff, exemplified the passive retreater. When a problem arose in staff meeting, Vicente became stone quiet. When asked for his input, Vicente would state his position in as few words as possible, then lapse into retreative silence again. As other staffers haggled over possible solutions, Vicente preferred the safety of hiding and refused to push his stated convictions. When his coworkers ignored his quietly stated ideas, Vicente's face clouded with wordless, sulking anger.

Thoughtless reactions against problems, either aggressive or passive, rarely lead to solutions, and in many cases they only exacerbate the problems. The Christian worker who persists in a mode of unprepared reaction will not be the positive force for problem solving he could be in the workplace.

Learn to Live Above Murphy's Law

Solomon wrote: "A man of knowledge uses words with restraint, and a man of understanding is even-tempered" (Prov. 17:27). The answer to problems on the job is not to fly off the handle or to crawl into a hole. It is the positive, helpful middle ground of thoughtful, controlled response. Make no mistake: Murphy's Law will strike repeatedly in the place where you work. But you can learn to live above pesky problems by preparing yourself with proper responses.

Prepare for Problems

The first line of response to problems is to expect them. Admit to yourself that things will go wrong at work. Replace your rigid "nothing should go wrong" idealism with flexible "Murphy is out to cause trouble" realism. Begin coaching yourself before the fact that you can and will positively respond to work problems instead of negatively reacting against them.

Several years ago, God encouraged me to pray myself into a state of readiness for the problems I faced daily. I began each day asking God to prepare me mentally, emotionally, and spiritually for the failures I would encounter that day. I specifically prayed that I would be able to welcome problems without reacting and that I would be ready to respond to them positively and properly. The result of that several-week prayer campaign was a heightened and confident readiness for impending problems.

Listen and Learn

Once we adopt a responsive mode to problems, we tend to think of ourselves as spring-loaded for action. A problem hits, and we're instantly ready to offer our wisest advice and roll up our sleeves to activate a solution.

But another key prerequisite for responding properly to problems is to listen before acting. Solomon reminds us: "He who answers before listening—that is his folly and his shame. . . . The heart of the discerning acquires knowledge; the ears of the wise seek it out" (Prov. 18:13, 15). We must discipline ourselves to listen carefully when a problem arises so that we can intelligently and sensitively work for the best solution.

Here are several specific guidelines for good listening in problem situations:

Listen all the way through. Your supplier calls to inform you that the ad merchandise you ordered for the October sale cannot be shipped until October 5, arriving at your store a week after the sale has started. You interrupt her explanation to express your displeasure at the delay, explaining that your customers will be expecting the merchandise to be on hand. The supplier continues with her apology, but you interrupt again, saying you need to call other suppliers right away—"So, good-bye." And you hang up.

You sampled enough of your supplier's message to understand the problem, but you snapped into responsive action without hearing her out. Your supplier was trying to tell you that she is sending a packet of manufacturer's rebate coupons for the sale merchandise by overnight mail. She is ready to compensate your customers for the delay by offering an additional $2.00 rebate on the sale price. But you hung up before you could hear the solution she had in mind.

Often we are so prepared to respond that we hang up on people, failing to listen to a problem situation all the way through. We hear just enough to prompt a rebuttal, an argument, or a hasty reaction. Instead, we need to listen patiently and openly to the whole story and examine the full scope of the problem. Again, Solomon's wisdom is appropriate: "It is not good to have zeal without knowledge, nor to be hasty and miss the way" (Prov. 19:2).

Monitor your own emotions. Whenever Murphy's Law strikes at your workplace, be sure to listen to your own emotional response to the problems and to those who cause them. Especially listen for defense signals that indicate that you are closing yourself to others in anger, frustration, or apathy. When you monitor and identify your emotions, you can counteract them through purposeful behavior.

For example, you can train yourself to periodically interpret the message you send to coworkers through your body language. When you find yourself sitting in a problem-solving meeting with your arms or legs crossed defensively, change your posture to convey openness. When you see yourself leaning away from the table apathetically, sit up straight or move your chair closer to the table to model interest. Do whatever you can to be sure your emotional response to a problem doesn't get in the way of a solution.

Accept the perspectives of others. One of the interrelational problems we often face is a difference of perspective. We are tempted to accept our ideas and solutions as right while judging the ideas and solutions of others as inferior, incomplete, or dead wrong. We are often stalemated in our collective responses to problems because we are closed to the insights and convictions of our fellow workers.

The discipline of listening in responding to problems requires that we explore the perspectives of others. First, we must be ready to say, "I accept that you have good reasons for feeling the way you do on this issue." Second, we must be ready to ask, "Why do you feel the way you do on this issue?"—and carefully listen to the response. As Solomon wrote, "The purposes of a man's heart are deep waters, but a man of understanding draws them out" (Prov. 20:5). When you open yourself to the perspectives of others, you just may discover a gold mine of solutions that outvalues the handful of nuggets you have found on your own.

Focus on the Solution, Not the Problem

My group at Tekronix was preparing to introduce a new product when the marketing manager stormed into a meeting. "We're supposed to start the training class on the new hardware," she growled, "and we don't have any training materials yet." She had a big problem, and since we were a team, we all had a big problem. We muttered about the people who had dropped the ball on the training materials. We grumbled about all the potential problems that might arise because the training materials were delayed. Before we realized it, we had wasted 45 minutes of valuable time crying over spilled milk, rehashing our big problem from a dozen different angles.

Sadly, our bad example is perpetuated daily in the workplaces of North America. Countless hours of constructive problem solving are sacrificed on the altar of needless problem rehashing. Yes, we should be prepared to analyze our problems in order to diagnose solutions. But all too often we get so absorbed in moaning about what *has* happened that we lose sight of what *needs* to happen.

When Murphy's Law strikes, the Christian worker should lead the way in focusing on the solution instead of the problem. When others are asking, "How could something like this happen? Who is at fault?" the Christian worker should be asking, "What is the central issue to be resolved? What will it take to turn it around and get it back on course? How many people and how much time and money is needed to correct the problem?"

You'll be surprised how quickly bad feelings can be diffused when the focus is shifted from problem sulking to problem solving. When creative energies are released on positive solutions, people start feeling good again. And the sooner the discussion is redirected from what *has* happened to what *must* happen, the sooner your work will return to a productive track.

Commit Yourself to Being Part of the Solution

When the air is filled with problem flak at work, you can choose to do one of three things: Sit back apathetically and watch the flak, jump in antagonistically and throw some flak of your own, or boldly cut through the flak and start working on a solution. The third choice—which is the right choice—takes commitment.

First, you must commit yourself *not* to perpetuate the problem by ignoring it or exacerbating it. Second, you must commit yourself to being part of the solution. And this commitment requires more than asking the right questions to reveal the needed solution. It also includes a commitment to roll up your sleeves and do what must be done to make that solution happen.

Are you ready to commit extra time and effort to assure that solutions to work problems are fully realized? It only takes one person at your place of employment who is fully committed to the solution to nullify the negative effects of Murphy's Law. You can be that one person.

Care Enough to Confront

One of the most difficult steps in problem solving is confronting the people who are part of the problem. Your subordinate is not fulfilling his job description. Your co-worker is getting sloppy on some of her inventory counts. Your employer is misleading the company execs about the costs of a project. As with other problems, you can choose either to grouse about the problem person or to lovingly confront him to affect a solution. The latter choice is the right choice.

Once my boss came to me and said, "I'm transferring Dick into your group because he's messing up in his present position. His team can't stand him, but his manager won't do anything about Dick's incompetence. I want you to fire him."

"You're transferring him into my group just so that I

will fire him?" I asked disbelievingly. My boss nodded.

"I can't do that," I said. "I'll give him a job, and if he messes up that job, I'll let him go. But I won't send him packing just because his manager can't handle him."

When Dick moved into my group, I sat him down for a personal heart-to-heart chat. I told him straightforwardly that he was here because he had alienated himself from his prior manager and team. I itemized his failures and promised that if he repeated them in his new job, I would do what his previous coworkers had insisted: terminate him.

Dick sat in wounded silence. "I didn't know I was such a problem," he said finally, without defending himself. "I thought I was doing OK. Nobody said a word to me."

Dick launched into his new assignment with a new perspective. He did a terrific job and became a good employee. During his first performance review, Dick said, "Jerry, I appreciate your honesty in confronting me about my failures. If it hadn't been for your openness, I might have lost my job." At that moment I could identify with Solomon's exclamation: "A man finds joy in giving an apt reply—and how good is a timely word!" (Prov. 15:23).

It is unfair not to confront someone who is contributing to a problem situation. As Christian workers committed to loving our coworkers, we are obligated to let them know exactly what's going on. To be sure, honest confrontation can be painful, and we may run the risk of straining relationships. But when confrontations are tempered with love, tact, and good timing, the odds of positive results are greatly in our favor.

Our confrontational message must be direct, clear, and accurate, never oblique. Unclear feedback only muddies the problematic waters, further obscuring the solution.

During one staff meeting, Jake, a project manager, presented his need for additional resources to complete his project. After some discussion, Jake's manager, Loren, responded, "Jake, I just don't feel comfortable about your resource needs." But Loren avoided specifics, and Jake left the meeting very frustrated and without a solution to his problem.

When I was alone with Loren, I asked, "Why are you uncomfortable about Jake's request for resources?"

"I don't have much confidence that Jake can get the job done," Loren admitted.

"You've got to tell him that," I insisted. "And you've got to outline for him what he must do to fulfill your expectations. Unless you confront him squarely about the problem, both Jake and the project will go down in flames, and it will be your fault."

When confronting a coworker about a problem, we must allow intellect to take the lead over emotion. Confrontation is not primarily the outpouring of feelings about the problem, although there may be some strong feelings to say, "Here's the way things are and here's the way they must be. What can I do to help?" Thoughtful confrontation will never lose sight of the primary goal: the solution of the problem.

QUICK FIX OR LASTING SOLUTION?

Often when responding to problems at work, we reach for the first workable answer instead of persisting for the best answer. When the machinery isn't working quite right, we tweak it back into adjustment but fail to fix it so that it won't break down again. When we keep receiving bad components from vendors, we box them up and ship them back without pursuing a solution that would eliminate the bad components altogether. Unfortunately, when we grab the first solution instead of persevering for the best solution, we end up solving the same problem again and again.

One of the most significant insights from Japanese technology we adopted at Tekronix can be summarized in one simple phrase: Solve the problem so that it can never occur again. When the once-for-all problem-solving mentality gained a foothold in our company, we saw some amazing solutions eradicate some long-standing problems.

For instance, we had a problem with plastic computer

terminal housings getting nicked and scratched as they rolled unprotected through the various stages of assembly. Many of the marred terminals were being rejected by quality assurance, costing the company piles of money.

Our problem-solving team was committed to finding a solution that would eliminate the problem completely. They realized that if the outside of the housing was protected during assembly and packing, it could not get damaged. So they devised a formfitting carrier made of foam and cardboard that fit snugly into the shipping box. Each plastic housing moved through the entire assembly process securely nested in its shipping carrier, completely impervious to damage from door to door.

On another front, many of our shipping clerks were suffering back injuries from moving heavy cases of hardware from one station to another. The quick-fix solution was to find stronger clerks and teach lifting safety, but the injuries persisted.

Again the focus of problem solving moved to eliminating back injuries completely. The result was the invention of a unique vacuum lift, an industrial strength vacuum hose that lifted each case by suction so that it could be moved with one hand.

The same principle of finding once-for-all solutions for product and procedure problems must also be applied to relationship problems. When you have difficulty getting along with a coworker, you can Band-Aid the problem by avoiding that individual or transferring to another department. But chances are there will be other people who will adversely affect you, and you will run from relationships throughout your career.

The Christian worker's goal in solving relationship problems is to strive for permanent solutions. Take the initiative to confront the people who bug you and lovingly pull all the hidden feelings out into plain sight. Find out what you can do to relieve interpersonal tensions and communicate your needs and wishes in the relationship.

Do You Have What It Takes?

What does it take to become a responsive problem solver in the work environment? First, it takes courage. It's difficult to respond positively to a problem when others are reacting negatively. It's difficult to introduce a solution when your coworkers want to wallow disconsolately in the problem. It's scary to confront coworkers at the risk of igniting anger or cooling a relationship. It takes courage to press ahead doing it right in the face of so many obstacles.

Courage is a human characteristic we all possess, but we must consciously activate it. God repeatedly urged Joshua to "be strong and courageous" (1:6, 7, 9, 18) as he stood on the brink of the problem-filled invasion of Canaan. Courage is not something we *do*; it's something we *are* that we willfully energize in our activities.

Second, it takes faith to become a problem solver. I must believe that there are solutions to be found for the problems I face at work. I must believe that God will honor my commitment to be His person on the job by guiding me to workable solutions. I must believe that if I act responsibly in the problem-solving process, God will use me to bring about the needed solutions. And I must believe that the solutions He reveals will contribute to the good of the company and its employees.

Third, it takes a lot of caring. You cannot be a committed problem solver on the job if you don't care about what you're doing or if you don't care about the people you're working with. The Christian employee should be marked by a pure love for his task and for those who are involved in it with him.

Do you have what it takes to be a responsive problem solver at work? Of course you do! Rely on the Holy Spirit to activate these qualities in you daily for His glory and your good.

· 5 ·

Hold Your Values Together

BURT, A CHRISTIAN SALESMAN, leads a weekly Bible study for coworkers in his company's lunchroom. After a Bible discussion on the topic of honesty, Molly, the company's bookkeeper and an inquiring non-Christian, approaches Burt privately.

"How can you say you're an honest Christian," she begins, slightly irritated, "when you pad your expense reports?"

"What do you mean?" Burt protests defensively, his face suddenly flushed.

"When you travel on company business, you're allowed to spend up to $35.00 per day for meals without receipts," Molly responds. "But I happen to know that you eat most of your meals at places like McDonald's. Yet your reports claim that you consistently spend over $30.00 per day for food. Do you really eat $30.00 worth of food each day?"

"Well, er, yes and no," Burt stammers. "I eat what I want, but I think I'm entitled to the full allowance if the company is willing to let me spend that much. Besides, it's common practice among salespeople these days."

"Even among Christian salespeople who say they believe in biblical honesty?" Molly persists, glowering.

"Molly, you've got to take into account that 20 cents a mile doesn't really cover the cost of my travel," Burt argues. "What I don't spend on food makes up for the mileage I don't—"

"I guess my husband was right all along," Molly interrupts as she starts to walk away. "You Christians are all a bunch of hypocrites."

No Two Ways About It

The scene above is fictional, but it represents countless factual episodes where a Christian's testimony in the workplace has been discredited by his less-than-Christian behavior. You may have been raised in a Christian home and possess a sterling church attendance record. You may have given thousands of dollars to missions and served on every committee in your church. But when you arrive on the jobsite every Monday morning, your Sunday Christianity doesn't really count for much. Most of your non-Christian coworkers couldn't care less about the time and money you have invested in your "religion." But they certainly will notice when your day-to-day actions around the office or shop don't jibe with your "holy Joe" talk or your Sunday-go-to-church reputation.

The core of the issue at hand is integrity. The Hebrew word for integrity is *tom*, meaning completeness, innocence, perfection, or uprightness. In King Solomon's day, *tom* was used to describe total honesty in the use of weights and measures by merchants. Solomon employed the term at least 10 times in Proverbs to describe the individual who is steadfastly committed to live righteously at every level of life experience.

The English word *integrity* comes from the same Latin root as *integer*, which refers to anything whole and complete in itself. In mathematics, an integer identifies a whole number, as distinguished from a fraction of the whole. For the Christian, integrity means a life committed to one God, one purpose, and one method of conduct—moral uprightness. The antithesis of the life of wholeness is a life of fragmentation—serving more than one god, entertaining multiple purposes, or operating under a moral code that changes to accommodate situations. Solomon captured the contrast in Prov. 11:3: "The integrity of the upright guides them, but the unfaithful are destroyed by their duplicity."

Integrity in the workplace means that your intentions, your words, and your actions are not unequal fractions but indistinguishable parts of a whole. Integrity describes the consistency of what you mean, what you say, how you say it, and how you behave. For the Christian worker, integrity means that there is no difference between the Sunday morning profession and the Monday morning expression of faith. Integrity means that the Christian values we believe, preach, and teach are identical to the values we live out in everyday business dealings.

Doris was a Christian secretary to a non-Christian executive. One day Doris buzzed her boss on the intercom to tell him he was wanted on the phone. He responded, "Tell him I'm not in."

"But sir," Doris interjected, "you *are* in. How can you ask me to say you are *not* in?"

The executive insisted that Doris get rid of the caller, but she refused. After dealing with the caller himself, Doris's boss stormed out to her desk and angrily demanded an explanation for her insubordination. "Sir, I am a Christian," she answered calmly, "and I do not ever lie. The fact that I will never lie *for* you should assure you that I will never lie *to* you."

That's integrity! Doris's internal commitment to the truth was matched by her words and actions. She acted as a whole, not as a collection of situational fractions.

Integrity's greatest reward is personal peace. When you only have one rule for your life, and you are consciously committed to living out your Christian values completely through your words and actions, you have nothing to hide. You don't have to worry that your non-Christian coworkers will find out that you're really a "holy Joe." You don't have to worry that your church friends will find out that you are secretly padding your expense reports or seducing your secretary. It's the peace of knowing that your life is transparent to God, to yourself, and to others, and that you have nothing to be ashamed of. As Solomon wrote, "The man of integrity walks securely, but he who takes crooked paths will be found out" (Prov. 10:9).

Don't Do as They Do

The greatest obstacle to expressing personal integrity in the work environment is the temptation we face daily to conform to duplicity in the work environment. Today's business ethics are largely based on situational morality. It's OK to lie to your customers or competitors, but not to your boss. It's OK to pad your expense report "within reason." It's OK to fudge on your specs as long as you still look better than others in the industry. It's OK to compromise your principles if it helps you achieve your personal work goals. It's OK to come in late and leave early if you get your work done. It's OK to talk dirty to coworkers as long as you don't go to bed with them. And it's OK to go to bed with them if you really love them.

Most of us spend at least 40 hours a week in an occupational microculture that accepts and promotes these negative values. Our Christian commitment to integrity struggles against the prevailing tide that insists that good and bad are relative to the circumstances. Certain inequities, injustices, improprieties, compromises, and errors are acceptable as long as we don't overdo them. We are urged—sometimes subtly and sometimes blatantly—to conform to fractured values in the face of the Scripture's clear directive: "Put away perversity from your mouth; keep corrupt talk far from your lips. Let your eyes look straight ahead, fix your gaze directly before you. Make level paths for your feet and take only ways that are firm. Do not swerve to the right or the left; keep your foot from evil" (Prov. 4:24-27).

The problem with tolerating a lot of "innocent" guidelines from our work microculture is the number of alternatives you face when making a decision. For example, the guidelines of Scripture clearly prohibit Christians from making sexual advances toward coworkers to whom they are not married. As a person of integrity, the Christian must only participate in interpersonal activities that are completely pure and well above moral temptation or suspicion.

But then there are the socially acceptable exceptions: It's OK for me to go out for dinner alone with my boss to talk business; everybody at the plant participates in "harmless" flirting or suggestive language; it doesn't hurt to get a little "touchy-feely" with coworkers of the opposite sex at a party or while celebrating a company achievement.

Suddenly, a potentially compromising situation arises, and I have too many options to sort through. "Is this an occasion for a harmless hug or should I settle for a handshake? Will he understand that my suggestive retort is not an invitation to my bedroom? Should I congratulate her for a job well done with a bonus in her pay envelope or a nice dinner out?"

Consider another scenario. As a Christian you are committed to speaking positively about coworkers, even when there is little good to be said. But others at your place of employment regularly talk derogatorily about other workers behind their backs. Comments about management are almost always negative and spiced with expletives.

You are in a lunchroom discussion where the foreman —who is not present—is being royally raked over the coals. All eyes turn toward you for your comments. If you are not firmly rooted in your commitment to respond positively, you may vacillate between some lesser alternatives or choose a tack you may later regret. What will you do?

Consider the Negative Results

Tolerating fractured thinking instead of striving for integrity in the work environment leads to many possibly negative results. First, your responses to moral dilemmas are marked by instability. You have accepted too many near-equal alternatives to be able to make stable choices. You tend to vacillate between unclear options.

Second, instability leads to indecision. You don't know what to choose, so you delay choosing or avoid choosing, deepening the dilemma. Sometimes your delay allows someone else to make the choice, perhaps a bad one.

Third, indecision results in unpredictability. Your coworkers are looking for predictability and dependability in the people they work with. The more incongruent your values are, the more incongruent your behavior will be, and the less comfortable and productive your coworkers will be working with you.

Fourth, instability, indecision, and unpredictability will lead to bad decisions. If you are unclear as to your moral response to the opposite sex in your workplace, you are in imminent danger of moral failure. If you are not rock solid in your commitment to truthfulness on the job, you will eventually perpetuate a half-truth or an untruth that could threaten your position or career. If you are shaky in your commitment to honesty, you will someday get caught with your hand in the company cookie jar.

Fifth, bad decisions and wrong decisions produced by your lack of integrity will earn you the distrust, disrespect, and lack of confidence of your superiors, peers, and subordinates. Without integrity, you rob your coworkers of the solid footing they need in their work relationship with you. Without integrity, your impassioned verbal witness for Christ on the job is futile and hollow.

A Foolproof Formula for Integrity

I don't believe any worker who is a Christian consciously chooses to forfeit his witness on the job through lack of personal integrity. But I have seen the witness of many Christian employees—including myself—tarnished because they did not choose activities that lead to the development of integrity. The formula for integrity is anything but a quick fix. It is a daily commitment and a lifetime quest. But if you will consciously apply yourself to the following disciplines over the long haul of your work experience, you will begin to reap the trust and respect of your fellow workers that leads to unbounded success as a witness for Christ.

Internalize God's Truth

There's no way around it: You will never establish yourself as a trustworthy and respected person of integrity apart from internalizing God's truth found in the Bible. In one of the few psalms not written by David, Asaph wrote of the king: "He [the Lord] chose David his servant . . . to be the shepherd of his people Jacob, of Israel his inheritance. And David shepherded them with integrity of heart; with skillful hands he led them" (78:70-72). Even though he experienced a sad moral failure, David is recognized as Israel's greatest king. What was his secret for leading Israel with integrity? Ps. 119:105 contains his personal testimony: "Your word is a lamp to my feet and a light for my path." A major key to David's success in his "career" as Israel's executive vice president was his attentiveness to God's Word.

Read God's Word systematically. Study God's Word aggressively. Memorize, meditate upon, recite, sing, and discuss God's Word. If possible, form a sharing group with other Christian working people and discuss specific applications of Bible principles to your work environment.

Clarify Your Value Base

Your value base at work consists of specific guidelines you establish for your conduct as an employee. A Christian's value base must be founded on the principles of God's Word and clearly identify practical expressions of those principles in everyday activities. For example, Doris, the secretary who wouldn't lie for her boss, had clearly established her value base in relation to truthfulness. Based on God's Word, Doris decided never to lie in her work setting. Once established, her commitment to truthfulness never needed to be made again, but merely implemented in each situation.

Truthfulness must be a part of the Christian's value base also, and the following chapter deals more specifically with that critical issue. The other chapter topics in this book reflect a Scripture-founded value base in the workplace—commitment, deference, quality of work, responsiveness, sacrifice, etc.

Furthermore, I have included in the Christian's value base some important predecisions in regard to integrity issues. For example, I do not take female coworkers out alone for meals. I try to extricate myself from conversations that are dominated by anger, gossip, or rumor. I confront as unprofessional coworkers who use excessive foul language. I will participate in discussions, but not in arguments. These values and others like them are the planks in a solid work environment platform. They constitute personal bylaws for behavior as a worker, established in advance to cover possible problem situations.

Your value base will continue to develop through the course of your work experience. Often a personal failure will bring into focus an area where you need to clarify a plank in your value platform. The more planks you set in place, the firmer your footing will be when you encounter those difficulties again.

As a Christian with a solid value base, you are well-equipped for positive and helpful decision making on the job. Having thought through moral issues and established a value platform, you don't need to wrestle through confusing alternatives. You have established solid moral guidelines that will serve as a reliable framework for decision making.

For example, you're in a meeting discussing price increases. The company's promotional material promises no more than a 5 percent increase per fiscal year. But some of your coworkers want to push through an 8 percent increase and move some numbers around to cover it up. As a person of integrity committed to honesty and truthfulness, you don't even need to deliberate the issue. "We promised no more than 5 percent," you insist confidently, "and if we go to 8 percent, we will break that promise. That's wrong, and I'm opposed to it."

Some issues you face may not be as clear as this example. But having thoughtfully and prayerfully prepared your value base, you will be miles ahead of those who need to decide right and wrong for every specific issue and decision.

Cherish Your Innocence

Paul's final instruction to the Roman Christians was, "I want you to be wise about what is good, and innocent about what is evil" (16:19). There are many temptations to evil where you work. As a Christian, you are not free to try everything your non-Christian coworkers feel free to try. You must be alert to the issues that are contrary to God's Word and make a conscious choice: "This is wrong: I won't do it."

To be "innocent about what is evil" means it's OK to choose against evil the first time you encounter it. You don't need to experiment with evil once or twice to know you should avoid it. You don't need to learn by your mistakes every time. For example, if some of your coworkers are hitting on cocaine, you don't need to see, touch, or taste the stuff. You are innocent of that evil; cherish your innocence and stay completely away from what you know to be wrong.

Or perhaps some of your coworkers wrongly help themselves to products or supplies. You may be the only one in your shop who doesn't take advantage of the situation. That's OK. Your innocence and integrity may someday be the witness one of your coworkers needs.

Strive for Consistency

The Christian employee has the distinct advantage of offering consistent, dependable values that many non-Christians cannot offer. And since integrity is perfected over the long haul, your consistency at maintaining your value base is a prime requisite for your development as a person of integrity. As your track record of consistency increases over time, you will find your coworkers eager to hear about the Christ who is the Center of your value base.

I enjoyed many gratifying rewards during my 23 years at Tektronix—promotions from my superiors, recognition from my peers, and loyalty from my employees. But my greatest personal fulfillment came from the many people at Tek who sought my counsel for both business and personal problems. "I feel I can talk to you," many of them said, "because your values are clear. I know I can trust you." I had the opportunity to assist and pray with many coworkers who had seen the character of Christ in my life.

But my witness on the job didn't just happen. It was the result of a career-long series of prayerful choices—some of them agonizing, some of them slow, and some of them wrong. But I can assure you that the pursuit of personal integrity promises spiritual rewards that transcend any career plateau you can envision.

· 6 ·

Remain True to the Truth

T HE BOSS HANDED ME the project schedule for the computer system we were developing. "I want you to
present this project schedule for me in the executive committee meeting, Jerry," Eric said.

I scanned the stages of the project and the dates for
completion he had entered on the report. "Eric, I can't
present this project schedule," I answered.

"Why not?" he quizzed.

"Because you and I both know that we can't make this
schedule. We're hopelessly behind; there's no way we can
meet these dates."

"I realize that," Eric answered. "But the execs need to believe we're close, or they'll be breathing down my neck."

"I understand your problem," I assured Eric, "but the report is misleading. It's not the truth, and I won't present it
as if it were." As you might guess, I wasn't very popular
with Eric for refusing his directive.

My experience with Eric and his report illustrates a
common challenge Christians face in the workplace today:
telling the whole truth in the prevailing atmosphere of
near-truth, half-truth, and untruth. Nothing can damage
your witness on the job more irreparably than your coworkers discovering that you withheld the truth from them.
And conversely, nothing can earn you more trust and respect from your coworkers than being identified as a consistent and thoroughly truthful employee.

Shades of the Truth

Everybody knows that Christians don't tell lies. After

73

all, the ninth commandment expressly forbids lying (see Exod. 20:16). Furthermore, Solomon said: "A false witness will not go unpunished, and he who pours out lies will perish" (Prov. 19:9). From our earliest days in Sunday School we have been drilled to tell "the truth, the whole truth, and nothing but the truth."

But most of the places where we work are a great distance from the Sunday School classroom. Though business ethics often reflect a pseudomorality that is somewhat biblical in nature, the commitment to total truthfulness in the workplace is often conditional at best. Few people tell blatant lies on the job—our coworkers wouldn't stand for it, especially if it affected their profit sharing. But many workers, including Christians, are guilty of veiling the pure white of total truth with the subtle gray of almost-truth. Compared to outright lies, these near-truths are close enough to the real thing to pass for white. But the standard for a Christian's communication is the purity of total, untainted truth. And contrasted to "the whole truth, and nothing but the truth," dingy, shaded truth is revealed for what it really is: a lie.

Christian workers are lured into shaded truthfulness by the same things that motivate some unconscionable non-Christian workers to cheat and steal on the job: the pressure to succeed. Often the competition for jobs, promotions, raises, and awards urges us to push ourselves upward in whatever way possible and grab for any advantage we can find. We want to communicate to our bosses and coworkers that we are more skillful, knowledgeable, reliable, efficient, resourceful, or profitable than the persons who want our jobs. So we subtly and sometimes subconsciously practice the following means of shading the truth to improve our image or position.

Exaggeration. We often resort to exaggerated overstatement to get attention or underscore a problem. We charge, "The quality defect on the new model is a disaster! It's going to cost us a million dollars in sales!" If we were totally truthful, we would say instead, "The quality defect is a problem that needs to be corrected soon. We have projected a $300,000 loss this year, but that figure can be reduced if we eliminate the problem right away."

We bluster, "I told you we should have ordered five more cases. We're sold out already, and at least a dozen customers are holding rain checks for the sale price." But if the truth were clearly stated, we would say, "We need to reorder right away. I have given out three rain checks, and I suspect that other customers may be asking for them."

Solomon said: "When words are many, sin is not absent, but he who holds his tongue is wise" (Prov. 10:19). Exaggeration is truth stretched out of shape by too many words. Exaggeration is distorted truth. As such it is not the real truth and should be eliminated from the Christian worker's communication. Jesus said: "Simply let your 'Yes' be 'Yes,' and your 'No,' 'No'; anything beyond this comes from the evil one" (Matt. 5:37). Our words should be simply and accurately truthful.

Fact manipulation. It's been said that you can make statistics say whatever you want them to say. Whenever we misrepresent the truth to our advantage by manipulating the facts, we are wrongly shading the truth.

Say, for example, that your boss wants to know what share of the auto oil filter market you have gained for the company. But the latest figures show your overall market share is way down from the previous year. An aggressive competitor has cornered the market on filters for imports and late-model domestic vehicles, pushing your firm into the shadows.

So in order to make a favorable impression, you segment the market to show statistical proof that your market share is up—for older domestic models. By skillfully rearranging the numbers—without actually changing them—you convince the boss that you are doing a good job, and thus you buy some time to recapture your lost markets.

Christian workers must be ready to let the facts say

what they say without shading the truth by manipulating them to their advantage.

Unspoken truth. Sometimes we become liars by withholding the truth when it should be revealed. Imagine that a coworker has inadvertently overlooked a minor assembly step before bringing the unit to your station. Taking the unit back to him will cost you some time and cut into your production quota. Allowing the defective unit to be discovered during quality inspection will make your coworker look bad and make you look good by comparison. You are tempted to keep quiet about the error as if you didn't know about it.

There is no difference between truth omitted and untruth committed. When you are aware of something that is important to the well-being of your company, of fellow workers, and fail to share it, you are shading truth that should be brought to light.

Excuses. Everybody makes mistakes on the job, but some people are unwilling to openly confess their goofs and admit responsibility for the problems they caused. Instead, they hide the real reasons for their failure behind a smoke screen of ostensibly valid excuses. For example, a secretary fails to complete a quarterly report in time for the board meeting. She failed principally because she underestimated the amount of time needed to complete the report. She started a few days later than she should have, allowed some less critical tasks to crowd into her schedule, and fell victim to some unforeseen emergencies that further delayed her.

"The sales VP needed some figures before leaving for a conference, the DP manager wanted me to test-drive a new word processor, and I was out two days with the flu," she explains to the board. She's telling the truth about the interruptions, but she fails to admit that it was her poor budgeting of time that was the real reason for her failure.

An excuse has been well-defined as the skin of a reason stuffed with a lie. At best, excuses are only partial truths, far below the standard of complete truthfulness God seeks in His people. We must be ready to implement the advice of Solomon: "He who conceals his sins does not prosper, but whoever confesses and renounces them finds mercy" (Prov. 28:13).

Subtle deception. Two weeks ago your boss gave you the latest copy of the trade journal, asking you to read three specific articles in preparation for staff meeting. The magazine stayed on your desk under a stack of more pressing tasks until the morning of the meeting. Two minutes before the meeting you hurriedly scanned the three articles, picking up a few key ideas so that you would have something to say about them.

Your boss opens the meeting by asking each staff member, "Did you read the three articles in the journal?" When she points to you, you answer, "Yes," and throw out a few key words from the articles to validate your response. In a technical sense, you rationalize, your response is correct. Your eyes glanced across all the print on each page. But are you answering the boss's question truthfully in the sense that was intended? Leading her to believe that you read the articles when you merely scanned them is a subtle and misleading deception.

Flattery. Flattery is excessive, untrue, insincere, or unwarranted praise employed as a lever for ingratiating oneself to the favor of another. We often call it "buttering up" the boss, supervisor, customer, etc. Again, flattering comments may be based on a shred of truth. For example, "the most creative advertising idea I've ever heard" may indeed be a workable solution. But overstating the truth or perpetuating a falsehood in order to gain approval or advantage is wrong.

Solomon's words add an interesting contrast: "He who rebukes a man will in the end gain more favor than he who has a flattering tongue" (Prov. 28:23). We must replace self-seeking flattery with sincere appreciation and compliments —and with confrontational rebukes when necessary.

What Is Truth?

One of the problems we have in communicating the truth in the work environment is our difficulty perceiving what the truth really is. Only God sees things the way they really are. The rest of us view everything and everyone through a series of subconscious filters that skew the truth to some degree. To whatever extent of distortion the truth appears to me through my personal filters, to that same extent the truth will be distorted when I act on it or pass it on to others.

For example, a new manager named Evan has been assigned to your branch. Evan has a reputation in the company for being a hatchet man—moving from branch to branch to trim the payroll of unnecessary employees.

Evan's history of heartless dismissals is strictly rumor in your branch; no one has worked for him before. But when Evan arrives, you are cool and defensive, avoiding all but the most necessary contact. You don't like him, you don't like working for him, and you are tempted to seek a transfer to another branch. Your attitude is obvious to Evan and your coworkers. Everything you say to him and about him is colored by your perception of him.

In reality, Evan is the most efficient manager in the chain. Profits have increased and costs decreased in each store he has managed. Evan's reputation as a hatchet man has been perpetuated by other managers in the chain who are disgruntled because Evan's skill, dedication, and efficiency has gained him the favor of the owners. Actually, Evan has only fired employees who were discovered to be cheating the company.

The difference between the real Evan and your distorted view of Evan can be found in three filters through which you perceived him. The three filters are biases, feelings, and motivations. We cannot help viewing people, circumstances, problems, and solutions through these three filters. Our challenge is to be aware that these filters exist within us and to allow God and His Word to purify these filters and minimize the distortion they tend to produce.

The Truth and Our Biases

A bias is a mental inclination or prejudice held toward a person, thing, event, or idea. Our biases shade reality with a combination of distorted facts and fantasies we already hold about the truth.

Your bad attitude toward Evan could be the result of one or more biases you subconsciously held against him. Perhaps Evan is a member of a different race that you have prejudged to be inferior to your race. Maybe Evan is younger than you, and you are biased against younger managers directing the work of older and wiser subordinates like yourself. Maybe you heard the rumors of Evan's cruelty from a former manager you admire, and you are biased in favor of this manager's evaluation. Or perhaps Evan is a Christian, but he attends a denomination you have judged to be less than evangelical, and you suspect him to be liberal.

Our biases come from our family upbringing, our formal education, our denominational distinctives, our political affiliation, and a number of other influences that crowd our minds with slanted ideas. Not all biases are wrong. But in order to see the truth clearly and communicate the truth in our work relationships, we must continually evaluate our biases in the light of God's truth, the Bible. Those biases that do not stand the scriptural test must be forfeited so that the truth may prevail in our work environment.

The Truth and Our Feelings

Another area that can shade the truth in your perceptions and your communication is your feelings about a person or issue. We are emotional creatures as well as intellectual creatures. Often, our unbidden feelings can cloud the facts, and our responses to people, events, or ideas spring from a picture of the truth that is tainted by our emotional state.

For example, your dislike for Evan may be rooted in fear. You're afraid that the hatchet man is moving to your branch to get you. You are paranoid that he is secretly watching your every move and listening in on your business calls, just waiting for an excuse to fire you. Your fear keeps you away from him and keeps you and those you influence from the truth about him.

Or perhaps your aversion to Evan is caused by envy. He has risen through the company ranks faster than you have. He is the big honcho, and you are a lowly peon. Since envy colors your relationship with Evan, a genuine kindness from him may be wrongly perceived as condescending patronage. You quietly withhold your support from him as a subtle protest against the advantages he enjoys over you.

Other feelings, such as anger, sympathy, hurt, or lust, can similarly filter the truth in your perception and your communication. As with biases, not all feelings are wrong. But we must continually examine our feelings and subject them to the truth instead of allowing the truth to be subjected to the misperceptions of our feelings.

The Truth and Our Motivations

A third filter through which the truth passes on its way to us and from us to others is our motivations. You can quickly identify your basic motivation in a relationship or task by asking yourself, "For whom am I primarily doing this—myself or God?"

If you are motivated by the gratification of selfish needs, you will evaluate the truth in terms of what you will get out of it. Continuing with our example of the new branch manager, your selfishly motivated response to Evan's hatchet-man reputation may be positive and hopeful. You eagerly plot how you can get on Evan's good side. You determine to look better than your coworkers so that they will get the ax instead of you. You anticipate some of your superiors being dismissed, making more room at the top for you.

But if your motivation is geared to glorifying God in the situation, your perception of the truth will be filtered through biblical values. Your primary concern will be for Evan and your coworkers instead of for yourself. Your responses will include words and deeds that make for the best working relationship in your branch, no matter what the cost may be to you.

CLEANING THE FILTERS

If you want to see objects clearly through glasses or a camera, you must keep the lenses clean. Any smudge on the lens will distort the picture. Similarly, you must keep the lenses of biases, feelings, and motivations as free as possible from obstructions that will impair your perception and communication of the truth.

How do we keep these truth-filters clean? A phrase from Jesus' prayer in John 17 gives us a helpful clue: "Sanctify them by the truth; your word is truth" (John 17:17). To be sanctified means to be set apart for God's special and sacred use. As Christian workers we desire to be special and sacred instruments who are useful to His purposes in our work environment. Jesus prayed that His followers would be set apart to His purposes through the truth of His Word.

The more committed we are to God's truth in His Word, the more clearly we will perceive and communicate the truth in our work situations and relationships. God's Word keeps the filters clean. Our continual, disciplined involvement in personal Bible study works like a cleansing agent, helping us to see things as they really are and call them as we see them. There is no substitute for God's Word in those who desire to be men and women of truth on the job.

Finding a Truthful Balance

The truth is like a scalpel. It can either be a precision instrument of healing or a slashing weapon of destruction. A trained surgeon can use a scalpel to save a life; a pathological killer can use the same instrument to end a life. Similarly, you can heal or hurt people with the truth. What makes the difference? With both the scalpel and the truth, the difference is in the intentions and skills of the persons who employ them. We want to be men and women of truthfulness in our places of employment, but we don't want to hurt people with the truth.

For example, my refusal to read Eric's misleading report to the executive committee was a stand I needed to take for the truth. But my confrontation about the report was personal between me and Eric. I could have taken the report to the meeting and said, "In the interest of the truth I want you all to know that the project schedule I am presenting today is basically a lie. We can never meet these dates, and Eric knows it." If I had approached the truth that way, I would have trashed my relationship with Eric and upset the executive committee unnecessarily. It would have been a hurtful and destructive use of the truth.

Two important qualities must balance your presentation of the truth at work. Think of yourself as a tightrope walker walking the wire of truth above a chasm of shaded truth or lies. You hold a perfectly weighted pole to keep you balanced securely on the wire. One end of the pole is love; the other end is wisdom.

Truth and love. Our commitment to be men and women of truth on the job must be balanced by our commitment to love our coworkers. Paul used this pithy phrase to describe the balance: "Speaking the truth in love" (Eph. 4:15). Love here is the familiar word *agapē,* which describes a selfless concern for the well-being of another. Our truthfulness must always be tempered by our concern for the well-being of our coworkers and customers. Otherwise, truth becomes a slashing knife instead of a healing scalpel.

As a manager I've confronted countless employees over the years on the quality of their work. During performance reviews I outlined each worker's strengths and pinpointed needs for improvement. Nobody likes to be called on the carpet to hear of personal failures and weaknesses. Such confrontations can be threatening and discouraging. So I endeavored to tell my employees the truth about their needed improvements in a positive way. I wanted them to come away from their performance review encouraged and challenged to do better, not defeated and discouraged. I tried to keep their best interest at heart and speak the truth in love.

Even when you stand alone confronting fellow employees who are not committed to the truth, you can do so with respect and kindness. In so doing you can even retain the trust and respect of those who disagree with you.

Truth and wisdom. Love must also be counterbalanced by wisdom in the life of the truthful worker. Wisdom will tell you how much must be said, when to say it, who must be included and/or excluded from a confrontation, and how you can excise falsehood without destroying your relationship with those who are disseminating it. For example, when I confronted Eric about his purposely misleading schedule, I did so alone. It would have been unwise of me to oppose him in the company of other employees. Eric may have interpreted a confrontation in a group as a ploy to discredit him publicly, and my point would have been lost in his feelings of anger or embarrassment.

It is always wise to evaluate your presentation of the truth in light of how it can achieve the greatest positive results with the least negative backlash. The person who observed that the truth sometimes hurts was correct; but like a healing surgery, the truth shouldn't hurt for long—it should heal. If your application of truth among your coworkers is doing more harm than good, you'd better check to see if you're wielding a hurtful butcher knife or a helpful scalpel.

· 7 ·

Give Till It Helps

ONE OF THE MOST GRATIFYING and fulfilling work experiences I enjoyed at Tektronix was managing the Unicorn project. The Unicorn was a low-cost graphics terminal we designed and manufactured that was very successful in a short period of time. The Unicorn project set new standards in our organization for efficiency of development time, reliability, and profitability. It was one of the most successful product lines in Tektronix's history.

There were two reasons for the overwhelming success of the Unicorn project. First, it was one of those occasions when we came up with the right idea at the right time. The market was ripe and ready for the Unicorn. Second, we had an extraordinary project team. Beginning with the original design and planning group and continuing through the engineering, manufacturing, and marketing groups, everybody was committed to the success of this project. Seventy people worked together for 18 months, assuring each other, "We'll do whatever it takes to make the Unicorn happen." They loved working with each other, and they made lots of personal sacrifices to reach the project goals.

Whenever a problem would pop up, several team members would voluntarily move in to solve it, sacrificing time and energy on their own tasks to help a fellow worker get through a rough spot. We even experienced a lot of crossover of helpfulness between groups. Engineers spent time investigating the problems unique to the manufacturing group and made changes in their designs to accommodate manufacturing's needs. Marketing solicited input from other groups on its unique challenges. Everyone accepted responsibility for every phase of the project and sacrificially gave himself to its successful completion.

In retrospect, I know that the camaraderie and teamwork we experienced didn't just happen. It was an attitude that my immediate staff and I worked to instill from the outset of the project. We started with a design and planning group of about 20 people. My staff and I knew each member of the group and maintained daily contact with them. When the engineering group started up, we spent time in their area daily.

As an administrative staff, our message to the early Unicorn project team was, "We're here to serve your needs and solve your problems. Whatever you need to do your job, just tell us and we'll get it for you." When someone had a need for a certain piece of equipment, we made sure the item was located and acquired as quickly as possible. We then hand-carried supply requisitions to the vice president's desk—and stood there until he signed them—in order to fill a team member's need quickly. We conveyed to our team that we would break our backs to ensure their success.

As our team swelled from 20 to 70, the attitude of sacrifice that we had modeled spread through the Unicorn project. Team members in every group bent over backward to meet each other's needs and solve each other's problems. They made the extra effort and traveled the second mile for each other. They subjugated their personal goals to the overall success of the team and the project. The result was an exceptional product and a rare sense of accomplishment shared by a close-knit team of 70 workers.

THE *AGAPĒ* FACTOR

For the non-Christians on our team (by far the majority), the sacrifices leading to Unicorn's success were primarily exercises in personal discipline. But for myself and other Christians, the sacrifices made were a positive expression of our goal to be Christlike in our character. I believe that a primary mark of the Christian on the job is the attitude and actions of personal sacrifice. Willingness to sacrifice personal time and effort for the good of company and co-workers is a practical expression of Christian love. Indeed, the root of *agapē* love—the highest form of biblical love—is sacrifice: "God so loved *(agapaō)* the world that he gave his one and only Son" (John 3:16). The supreme example of love in the history of mankind is the sacrifice of Christ on the Cross to solve our eternal sin problem.

Those of us who are the recipients of Christ's sacrificial love are also to be the perpetuators of that love. He left us not only an example to follow but also a command to obey: "If anyone would come after me, he must deny himself and take up his cross and follow me. . . . If anyone wants to be first, he must be the very last, and the servant of all" (Mark 8:34; 9:35). As a Christian, I am placed in my work environment to sacrifice myself for others. It's not an option, it's my very identity. Sacrifice is what Christians are all about. As a Christian on the job, I must occupy the role I have inherited from my Savior to be the daily servant of my superiors, my peers, and even my subordinates.

What About My Rights?

Often when God lays down the law for our behavior, we tend to look for the loopholes. When Jesus said our sacrificial love is to be boundless—as the servants of all—we start erecting boundaries to excuse ourselves from sacrifice in some areas.

As a stockman, you notice that one of the cashiers is having difficulty installing a new cash register tape. She asks you to help her. You have replaced tapes before, but replacing tapes is a cashier's job. Besides, you have more than enough stock work to keep you busy your entire shift. Every minute you spend helping her will put you another minute behind on your own tasks. Register tapes are not my responsibility, you rationalize, so I don't have to do it. It's not in my job description. I have a right to do my own work without interruptions like this.

But in reality, servants don't have any rights. They exist

only to fill the needs of those they serve. I can almost hear God saying, "I don't care if it's in your job description or not. If you have an opportunity to serve your coworkers, you are duty bound to serve them." Jesus excluded no one from His sacrifice; we are to exclude no one from ours.

Of course, the call to serve others does not negate the call to serve your employer by faithfully completing your job responsibilities. You're not just a floating angel of mercy looking for others to help while your tasks go ignored. You are called to be the best at your own tasks *and* serve others where you have the opportunity. You may need to arrive at work a little early, stay a little late, or work through some coffee breaks. That's the crux of sacrifice.

What About My Feelings?

You're dog tired. You've already spent an extra 45 minutes cleaning up some paperwork after a grueling day. You suspect a touch of the flu coming on, and you can't wait to get out the door and head home.

But you can hear the janitor down the hall trying to move some tables in the conference room so that he can clean the carpets. The tables are unwieldy for one person, and you know he could use a hand getting them folded and stacked. But *I'm bushed, and I think I'm a little ill,* you groan to yourself. *Harvey is so talkative, he'll probably want to stand around gabbing for half an hour. I just don't feel like helping him today.* You have suddenly quantified *agapē* service in terms of how you feel.

If Jesus had followed His feelings when facing the sacrifice of the Cross, we would still be unredeemed. The humiliation and agony of a criminal's execution was not what Jesus felt like experiencing on Good Friday. Yet He personified sacrificial *agapē,* and so He fulfilled His mission of redemption solely because the Father had ordered it and we needed it.

A servant's personal feelings about his responsibilities have no bearing on whether or not he completes his work. "I don't care whether you feel like serving or not," Jesus calls to us. "Your loving service is to spring from obedience, not from emotion."

What About My Pride?

We have all worked with people we don't like, or with those who don't like us, or both. Personality clashes and job rivalries are common, creating tensions that sometimes strain the limits of our Christian love. Some coworkers overtly or covertly oppose us simply because we are committed to a Christian work ethic that makes us look good and makes them look bad.

It is for these people, too, we are called to serve. In Matt. 5:43-48, Jesus suggested that loving service to those who oppose us is the real proof of love. Anybody can love someone he likes and who likes him. The true test of Christian love is to sacrificially love and serve our rivals or enemies on the job with as much fervor as we serve our friends.

"But that person has gossiped about me, hurt me, undercut my authority, and resisted my friendship," we say. "I'll sacrifice to help my friends, but not to give my enemy an advantage. I have my pride."

Again I hear the voice of Christ, our Model, without a tinge of sympathy, saying, "I don't care what your coworkers have said about you or done to you. Your assignment is the same: Lay down your life to help them succeed in their job tasks." Pride and sacrifice are as incompatible as water and oil.

What About My Track Record?

I've known a lot of people who made many sacrifices over the years for the success of their company and for their own individual projects. They loaded the front end of their experience with voluntary overtime and extra contributions. But as their careers became established, they declared, "I've put in my time and paid my dues. I don't need to make big sacrifices anymore. It's time the company made a few sacrifices for me." They rationalized that sacrifice has a time limit. It's a good thing to do for a while, but you don't need to make a lifetime habit of it.

Time is another boundary we erect to limit the expression of *agapē* service to our fellow workers. We let ourselves off the hook by saying, "I helped him out of a jam the last three times; let somebody else help him this time." Or we complain, "She never appreciates the sacrifices I make to help her. It's time to let her see how hard it will be without me." We arbitrarily decide how far our sacrificial service will go in a given relationship or task.

But, by definition, *agapē* has no such borders. Like forgiveness, loving sacrifice is not to be limited by the clock, the calendar, or a certain number of occurrences. "I don't care how many times you have sacrificed yourself to help someone without reward or recognition," Jesus seems to be saying to us. "Sacrifice is to be an endless characteristic of your Christian life-style in the workplace."

AGAPĒ IS SOMETHING YOU DO

Someone once said, "It's amazing what can be accomplished when you don't care who gets the credit." As the saying suggests, personal sacrifice—especially forfeiting personal recognition—is a doorway to getting things done. And that's a key to the sacrifice that springs from biblical *agapē:* Sacrificial love is something you do. It's not just a warm feeling for others, nor is it lip service on a par with glib expressions like, "Have a nice day." Sacrificial *agapē* love is a verb—action that must be seen, heard, and felt by the people who work with you.

Active *agapē* will be communicated to your fellow workers in at least four ways. First, your words and deeds should openly state your availability to serve. Your co-workers should hear the message clearly every day: "I'm willing to drop everything and lend a hand when you need me." Often you won't know where and when you can serve someone unless your availability convinces them to seek out your help.

Second, availability must be backed by responsiveness. When an opportunity for service arises, you must respond as you said you would. Claims of availability are quickly reduced to meaningless platitudes if there are no responsive actions to substantiate them.

Third, your commitment to serve will be communicated through your support. The servant-worker is not climbing to the top of the organization to be a figurehead, but burrowing underneath the organization to be a pillar of support. Your coworkers need to know that you are supportive of them and their efforts by sacrificially lending your brains and brawn to help them reach their work goals.

Fourth, your role as a peer-servant will be observed through the affirmation you provide for your coworkers. Appoint yourself to be a P.R. committee of one with the task of making sure your coworkers get the recognition and acknowledgment they deserve for their efforts. Write them cards, letters, or memos of appreciation. Mention their accomplishments in staff meetings and around the water cooler or lunch table. Serve each person's need for a positive self-image by being a fountain of genuine affirmation to them and about them to others. We will discuss this facet of loving service in greater detail in chapter 10.

PREPARING FOR DAILY SACRIFICES

Availability, responsiveness, support, and affirmation are like the major stones in the altar of our commitment to be men and women of sacrifice on the job. But each day we place ourselves on that altar in a variety of specific ways. Let's identify some of the day-to-day sacrifices that Christian workers must be ready to make.

It's a Dirty Job, But . . .

Each occupation seems to have a unique handful of crummy tasks that nobody likes to do. These dirty jobs range from difficult to unglamorous to tedious to mundane. Do you remember Ed and the trash room? No matter how exciting and fulfilling our careers may be, we can't seem to rid ourselves completely of the nagging little jobs that we wish would just go away.

Sacrifice on the job means stepping forward to do the

lousy jobs that everyone else avoids. For example:

• Your entire staff is invited to attend the January sales conference in West Palm Beach—all expenses paid. But somebody needs to stay behind in snowy Minneapolis to mind the store. Even though a junior member could be forced to take the home office duty, you volunteer to stay and work so that others may go and play.

• The janitor at your machine shop has quit, and your budget-conscious manager is not hurrying to hire another. In the meantime the employee rest rooms are neglected and getting dirtier by the day. You quietly assume responsibility to arrive at work 20 minutes early to make sure they are clean and stocked with paper supplies for the day.

• The receptionist is supposed to do the filing in her spare time, but she can barely get away from the switchboard for coffee breaks, let alone filing. Everybody else ignores the growing stack of folders that threatens to inundate the office. You decide to stop and file five folders every time you are near the cabinet, and spend a few minutes after hours helping the receptionist finish the filing for the day.

Some of the sacrifices involved in dirty jobs are relational in nature. Someone on the assembly line is sending consistently sloppy work downline. Your boss's drinking problem is dragging his whole staff down with him. A coworker is tapping the till, cutting into everyone's profit margin. Somebody needs to risk rejection and wrath to stand up for the right by confronting people in the wrong. It's a dirty job, but somebody—namely the Christian worker committed to *agapē*—has to do it.

It's Hard to Be Humble

Sometimes we can identify with the country-western singer's comic lament, "O Lord, it's hard to be humble when you're perfect in every way." Work is going well, promotions and raises are on schedule, and the sky's the limit in our chosen field. We're tempted to wave good-bye to our coworkers as we zoom by them on our way to the top.

But because of our Christlike nature as servants, we are to be at least as committed to the success of our coworkers as to our own success. We are called to lay our pride on the altar in order to make others successful. In some cases, we may need to sacrifice some of our self-centered goals in order to assure the success of our coworkers. A sacrificing servant will be ready to do so even when he receives no acknowledgment for the good deed.

Say, for example, that you and a coworker suggest different but equally workable solutions for a job-related problem. You know that the idea that is implemented will result in significant recognition for its originator. You would enjoy the approval of your peers and superiors, and the credits on your résumé wouldn't hurt either. But you are called to work for the success of others also. The choice is yours. You can selfishly push your own idea or humbly step back and support someone else's idea, allowing him to enjoy the success of the moment. The *agapē* servant will continually watch for ways to lift others to success and prominence even at the expense of personal accomplishment and notoriety.

Sacrificing for the success of your superiors is one thing; sacrificing for the success of your peers is another. Your boss expects you to work hard and sacrifice for the good of the company. Let's face it: Your diligence and service in his employ are your meal ticket. The better your boss looks because of your work, the better your chances are for advancement.

But your peers on the job are often your rivals for promotions, raises, and awards. Sacrificing for their success may not gain you anything but a longer wait for the next promotion. Serving your peers, therefore, is where humility and personal sacrifice really come into focus. *Agapē* is selfless love that expects nothing in return. Expressing loving service to your equals on the job is the greatest sacrifice because they often cannot or will not reciprocate, and they may even take advantage of your "weakness."

When It's Time to Bail Out

Sometimes the sacrificing servant on the job must decide to hang in there even when it's time to bail out. For instance, the company is in financial trouble, and other employees are seeking employment elsewhere to avoid going down with the ship. But your commitment to the firm challenges you to sacrificially support the ownership in the face of possible layoffs or bankruptcy.

Or say that a coworker has an obvious drinking problem that threatens her job. Some of her friends at work have cut her off, fearing that they will be judged guilty by association. The general opinion is, "Give her enough rope to hang herself, then we'll all be rid of a problem." You know that you will be ridiculed for helping her conquer the problem and retain her job. But as a servant, you are ready to sacrifice the approval of the group to stand by someone in desperate need.

The risks of hanging in there when it's time to bail out are great. You could lose your popularity, your money, or your position. But in reality, a servant has nothing to lose. Anything that seems to belong to the servant actually belongs to the master. As servants of a heavenly Master with limitless resources, any losses we may suffer during sacrificial service to others can be easily recouped. We are in the care of a beneficent Master who will meet the needs of those who serve Him faithfully.

I DID IT AND I'M GLAD

I think God has equipped us with an internal reward mechanism that is activated when we obey His call to be loving servants in the work environment. I have experienced the satisfying joy that comes from sacrificially giving myself for the good of my fellow workers. It just feels good to know that we have done the right and loving thing in a task or a relationship. It's the inner witness from the Holy Spirit that we are in sync with Christ's sacrificial nature.

Conversely, I know the inner pain that results from

pridefully pushing my success ahead of the needs of others. It's a bad feeling, an uncomfortable feeling. It's the inner signal from the Holy Spirit that our goals and God's goals are out of alignment, that we have wrongly served ourselves instead of Him and others.

Having experienced both the ecstasy of doing right and the agony of doing wrong, I am encouraged to press on as a servant to Christ in the workplace. Furthermore, I have the promise of Scripture that my *agapē* endeavors do not go unnoticed. Our Lord promised, "He who humbles himself will be exalted" (Luke 18:14). Our goal is humility, sacrifice, and service to others before the Lord. Our reward is the guarantee that God will lift us to a position of His choosing.

Agapē on the Job

First Corinthians 13 is commonly called the "love chapter" of the Bible. *Agapē*—the Greek word for selfless, sacrificial love—occurs nine times in the 13 verses of the chapter. Paul's description of *agapē* is both poetic and intensely practical, inspiring us and equipping us to selfless service of others.

The following paraphrase of 1 Cor. 13:4-8, based on the *New International Version* (used throughout this book), tailors Paul's timeless words to the opportunities and challenges we face as Christians in the non-Christian workplace. These lines reflect the standard of selfless love that we must demonstrate to win the trust and respect of our coworkers.

Love is patient with overbearing bosses and underachieving coworkers.

Love is kind when others take credit for your ideas or solutions.

Love does not envy the accomplishments and advancements of others in the company.

Love does not boast of personal accomplishments and advancements.

Love is not proud of position, salary, or advantage.

Love is not rude to subordinates.

Love is not self-seeking in corporate efforts or shared responsibilities.

Love is not easily angered when projects or people don't pan out as planned.

Love keeps no record of wrongs suffered at the hands of fellow workers, customers, vendors, or competitors.

Love does not delight in evil suffered by fellow workers, customers, vendors, or competitors.

Love rejoices with the truth, even when the truth is uncomplimentary to a personal work record.

Love always protects superiors, peers, and subordinates.

Love always trusts superiors, peers, and subordinates.

Love always hopes for the best in superiors, peers, and subordinates.

Love always perseveres through the failures of superiors, peers, and subordinates.

Love never fails, even when everything and everyone on the jobsite turns against you.

· 8 ·

Let Bygones Be Bygones

FOR A COUPLE OF YEARS I occupied a marketing role in a product group. Our job in marketing was to assess the marketability of our group's products in order to assure their success in the marketplace.

I remember two electronics products that came through the pipeline at the same time. To me, the first one looked like a real winner, well worth taking to market. I supported the product enthusiastically, and our marketing efforts were met with solid success. The second product I judged to be poorly conceived—the wrong idea at the wrong time—and I opposed taking it to market. But the engineers were strongly in favor of the product, and the division manager sided with them and overrode my opposition. The product went to market and failed miserably, just as I had predicted.

Almost eight years later, while I was managing another product group, I interviewed a veteran engineer named Cal for a position in my group. Cal had been one of the engineers on the ill-fated project I had opposed years earlier, which for me was only a faint memory.

As the interview began, Cal—a Christian man—seemed uneasy and standoffish. Then the dam burst. Cal unloaded some feelings he had been carrying for almost eight years. "You never liked our product, and you didn't give it a fair chance," he boiled. "You were the hatchet man sent to kill our product. I don't know how a Christian executive like you could be so negative and destructive." As Cal talked, I was astonished that he had kept the issue—which was long dead and buried—simmering in his memory.

After Cal had dumped his load and cooled down, I reminded him that the product I had opposed was not scuttled in the boardroom but in the marketplace. The product *did* go to market and was rejected by the consumer. "That's why I opposed it," I concluded. "I wasn't against you or anyone else who worked on it. I just knew it wasn't a good idea, and the product's dismal showing proved me right."

As we continued to talk, Cal sheepishly admitted that his long-festering grudge had blocked him from a relationship with me as his Christian coworker. Finally he apologized, and we grasped hands in agreement that we had resolved our differences—which up till then I had no idea existed. I eventually hired Cal, and we became good friends and supportive Christian brothers.

HOLDING ON WHEN YOU SHOULD LET GO

In the dog-eat-dog working world, where corporate profits and personal success are on the line every day, it's easy to be offended by your coworkers. Your male boss promotes an attractive female rival even though you have seniority. You are inadvertently excluded from an important policy-making meeting. The scatterbrained paymaster keeps messing up your payroll deductions. Word processing is always misspelling your name on your dictated business letters. The mechanic in the next bay borrows your tools without asking. The salesperson in the adjoining cubicle talks so loud that you can't concentrate on your own work.

Most offenses we suffer are inadvertent—as when I unintentionally offended Cal by discouraging the marketing of his pet project. Other offenses are intentional and designed to annoy, discourage, hurt, or destroy. An envious coworker falsely accuses you in front of the boss in order to discredit you and draw attention to herself. Your foreman harasses you because you won't go drinking with the guys after work. Another salesperson purposely calls on customers in your territory behind your back. Needing a scapegoat, your boss unjustly blames you for slumping numbers and demotes you or fires you.

Few of us are seriously offended by our subordinates. After all, employees usually try to keep on the better side of their employers. But all of us are occasionally offended by our peers and superiors at work—those who don't need to please us in order to keep their jobs. Everyone at your level and above has the capacity to let you down or mess you up, sometimes even to the extent that your career is jeopardized.

How should we respond to the people at work whose unintentional offenses tempt us to lose patience or whose intentional attacks threaten our job security? For the Christian, the biblical answer is clear: Forgive. You don't need to know any more scripture than the Lord's Prayer: "Forgive us our debts, as we also have forgiven our debtors" (Matt. 6:12). As repentant sinners, we desire and expect God to forgive our sins. As the great Forgiver, God expects us to forgive those who offend us.

The issue of forgiveness was so important to Jesus that He returned to the topic at the close of His model prayer: "If you forgive men when they sin against you, your heavenly Father will also forgive you. But if you do not forgive men their sins, your Father will not forgive your sins" (Matt. 6:14-15). And in the parable of the unmerciful servant (18:21-35), Jesus revealed that forgiveness toward those who offend us is to be open-ended, not restricted by any number of offenses.

The definition of the Greek word for forgiveness in the New Testament, *aphiēmi*, leaves little doubt as to what we are to do with each offense. Literally translated, the word means to forget it, drop it, give it up, leave it behind. The same word describes Peter and John *leaving* their nets and their father to follow Christ (Mark 1:18-20), and Jesus *yielding* His spirit to die on the Cross. Wherever it is used, *aphiēmi* describes the general action of letting something go.

And that's just where the problem lies with us, isn't it? Instead of letting go of the offenses of others, we hold onto them. The negative deeds and words that others direct toward us—either intentionally or unintentionally—are like stones being thrown at us. Our natural tendency is to catch the stones and hold them until we have an opportunity to throw them back at our opponent vengefully. But Christ challenges us to let the stones bounce off us and then ignore the temptation to pick them up and either store them like ammunition or throw them back.

When your hands are full of stones, you are unable to use your hands to help others or care for others. Similarly, when your heart holds on to the offenses you suffer instead of letting them go in forgiveness, your inner capacity for Christlike love is diminished. Bitterness, anger, and plots of retribution occupy space where compassion should be thriving. We must allow all stones of offense to fall harmlessly out of our hands and leave them behind in our pursuit of a life-style of love toward those who offend us.

Holding Patterns

Sometimes it is difficult to tell if we have let go of our coworkers' offenses or if we are subconsciously holding on to them. We may trick ourselves into believing we hold no grudges, when one or more of the following manifestations reveal an attitude of unforgiveness:

Sniping. Freida was an extremely talented engineering manager who worked for me for a while. During one of our projects, the engineering division was under tremendous pressure, and I needed to schedule a strategy meeting with Freida and her team. Due to her travel schedule, Freida was not available to attend the meeting, but we agreed that I should go ahead with the meeting in her absence.

As it turned out, the meeting I scheduled had to be postponed. When I rescheduled the meeting with the engineers, I wrongly assumed that Freida was still unavailable on the date I selected. I went ahead with the meeting without notifying Freida, not realizing that she was on campus at the time.

When Freida heard what I had done, she was really upset, thinking I had purposely excluded her from the meeting. But she never said a word to me about the oversight, and I went on believing she was out of town on the day of the meeting. But I did notice a change in Freida. Over the next several weeks she was uncharacteristically irritable. She chipped, griped, and grumbled about inconsequential matters, and somehow I felt her complaints were off-handedly directed toward me. Finally, I called her in to confront her about the subtly hostile behavior. When I discovered that my inadvertent oversight was at the root of her problem, I apologized, and the air between us was immediately cleared. But who knows how long I might have been the target of Freida's grumbling if I hadn't approached her.

I call Freida's style of responding to an offense sniping. Sniping is common, everyday grumbling that characterizes someone who has been rubbed the wrong way and can't let go of the offense. Sniping is not a direct frontal attack, but a long-distance potshot from the bushes that is difficult to pin down. It is subtle retaliation, more like stinging an offender with pebbles than taking aim with a large stone.

If you find yourself irritated with a coworker and you express that irritation through grumbling and complaining, you may be holding a grudge that needs to be dropped. Sniping comments should be a red flag alerting us to a possible attitude of unforgiveness that must be dealt with.

Cold war. Sometimes our attitudes of unforgiveness are camouflaged under a response of passive retaliation, a cold war of nonverbal anger. Someone has offended you, so you get back at him by quietly excluding him from your life. You ignore him at a meeting, avoid him at coffee break, withhold recognition or compliments, and cut all lines of communication except those that are absolutely necessary to sustain the working relationship.

In a cold war relationship between coworkers, it's not what you say and do that reveals a wrong attitude, it's what you *fail* to say and do. For example, if you customarily wander through the shop, saying hello to your coworkers before work, but find yourself avoiding someone who offends you, you may be holding a grudge against that person. Or if you are physically affectionate with your staff—frequently shaking their hands or patting them on the back—but find yourself withholding your affection from someone, you may be harboring unforgiveness that must be confronted and resolved.

Disguised retribution. Gavin, George, and I were on the same product team for a period of time. Gavin was a real pusher, often trying to steamroll the staff with his favorite programs. On one occasion he had convinced half the team to go with him on an idea, but George and I felt strongly that Gavin's plan was not right for us. The harder Gavin drove the staff to adopt his program, the harder George and I stood against it. Eventually, we turned the tide against Gavin's idea.

For the next two or three months, Gavin opposed everything George and I contributed to the staff. Every idea we suggested was a dumb idea. Every solution we advanced was unworkable. It didn't matter what the subject was; if George and I were for it, Gavin was against it. He even told a group of sales managers in our presence, "We can't implement this idea because George and Jerry don't want any programs that will help us."

Gavin's response to behavior that he considered offensive could be called disguised retribution. He was getting back at us through cruel verbal jabs and embarrassing putdowns. His barbs seemed aimed at our ideas, but he was really blasting us as persons. Even if George and I suggested the best possible solution to a problem, Gavin would oppose it because he was committed to getting us for getting him.

If you find yourself gunning down an idea or solution because you are angry at the person who suggested it, you may be holding on to an offense that you must release through forgiveness. Not only will your grudge block you from a fruitful relationship with that person, but also you may find yourself foolishly throwing away some good ideas he suggests.

Bookkeeping. Sometimes we don't retaliate against those who offend us—at least not right away. Instead, we keep a running mental ledger of offenses, quietly itemizing each coarse remark, bad decision, or selfish power play. Each offense is like an item of evidence that is collected and held for the right moment. We slowly and deliberately build a case against that person until we can bring him to "trial," either leveling him personally with a flood of collected grievances or mustering him out of the division or the company by dumping the evidence in front of our superiors.

I remember an example of bookkeeping exhibited by a new boss. The first question Wendell asked when he came in to take over the division was, "How is Thad doing?" Thad was one of my engineers and a friend.

"He's doing OK under the circumstances," I answered.

"Isn't he behind schedule?" Wendell pressed.

"Yes, but it's a tough project," I admitted. "It would be difficult for anyone to stay on top of our grueling schedule."

Wendell looked away thoughtfully. "Thad may not be the right guy for this job," he said.

I was momentarily perplexed at Wendell's dissatisfaction with a man who was doing a very good job with a very tough project. But as Wendell continued to talk, I realized that he had been keeping books on Thad from an event that happened nearly two years earlier. For a time, Thad's wife, Faye, worked for Wendell when he was the vice president of another organization. After she had moved out of his group, Faye ran into Wendell and some of his friends at an electronics show. She used the chance meeting as an opportunity to chew out Wendell royally—in front of his friends—for mismanaging their group.

Wendell was unable to retaliate for the embarrassing incident because Faye was no longer in his organization. But he kept the event alive in his memory and welcomed the opportunity to become Thad's boss and build a case against him.

Shortly after my conversation with Wendell I met with Thad. "Wendell wants you out," I warned. "I'll protect you as much as I can, but you had better watch your step."

Thad did make some mistakes during the project that,

considering the pressure he was under, could have been excused—but not by Wendell. Every misstep was evidence in Wendell's attempt to prosecute Thad as payment for his wife's criticism. Wendell kept pressuring me until I had no alternative but to help Thad relocate to another group.

Do you find yourself reliving past offenses by coworkers and relishing the thought of getting even? Paul wrote that love *(agapē)* "keeps no record of wrongs" (1 Cor. 13:5). As Christian workers, we are commanded to let go of any and all offenses we are tempted to collect as evidence against others. Mental ledgers of wrongs suffered must be shredded by actively forgiving and forgetting each entry.

The Price of Holding On

Whenever I fail to obey God's directive to live in forgiveness toward coworkers who offend me, I risk running up a staggering physical, social, and spiritual "bill." The Christian's new nature is engineered by God to operate most efficiently when it is not carrying the unnecessary baggage of unforgiven offenses. When we continue to carry what God has told us to leave behind, we may end up paying a steep price for our stubbornness.

The physical price. When I was fired as the project manager of one of Tek's groups, I held a grudge against my ex-boss for a long time. Instead of dousing the sparks of bitterness, anger, and hatred the event prompted, I fanned them into a raging blaze through unrelenting contempt.

As a result of my unforgiveness, I was affected physically. I couldn't sleep at night. My hands developed a slight tremor. I became a flinching bundle of raw nerves until I consciously let go of the offense through persistent prayer and specific words and actions of forgiveness.

If your hand comes into contact with a flame and you fail to withdraw it, you will get burned. Your body was not designed to survive such abuse without pain and damage. Similarly, you cannot hold on to the hot coals of unforgiven offenses without paying a physical price. Bitter, vengeful attitudes will burn through your soul and eventually cause physical pain and illness.

The social price. Your primary role among your co-workers is to be an encourager and a witness. But failing to let go of others' offenses will drive a wedge between you and the people God has called you to serve. You will think of yourself as superior to those who wrong you, and consequently you will exclude them and devalue them. A prevailing attitude of disrespect toward offending coworkers will keep you from effectively impacting them for Christ.

The spiritual price. God's thoughts on the subject of offenses suffered are clear: Let them go. To whatever extent we selfishly begrudge those who wrong us, to that same extent unforgiveness eclipses our relationship with God. Unforgiveness gives rise to pride. Instead of humbling ourselves before others, we toot our own horn, trying to rebuild the self-image damaged by the offenses of others. And unforgiveness spawns ungratefulness. We resist thanking God for the difficult situations and relationships He allows for growth in our lives.

Unforgiveness will bankrupt you physically, socially, and spiritually if it continues unchecked. That's too high a price to pay, especially when God has promised to avenge justly any wrongs we suffer (see Rom. 12:17-19).

Tips for Releasing Your Grip

The key to letting go of the offenses you suffer from others is never grabbing onto them in the first place. Hurtful words and deeds, whether intentional or unintentional, should flow through us like sand through open fingers. The following two tips may help keep you from clinging to unforgiving thoughts and deeds.

Covenant with God to let go. Becoming a person of forgiveness in your working world is first a matter of choice and commitment. You need to promise God that, to the best of your ability and with His help, you will let go of every offense you suffer. No matter how great the urge to catch and hold the stones thrown at you, covenant with God that you will not do it. Once you make a lifetime commitment to forgive, you don't need to make it again in specific circumstances; you merely need to apply it. Once you establish the standard of what you will do, you simply need to act in accordance with your standard.

Does making a covenant with God mean you will never hold a grudge again? Of course not. We are weak, we make mistakes, we fail in our commitments. But when God and I agree that I will be a forgiving person and I fail my commitment, God will call me into account. He lovingly turns my attention back to our agreement. As soon as I am aware that I have departed from the standard, I confess my sin and return to my chosen posture of forgiveness toward all who wrong me.

Covenant with God not to retaliate. Just as God and I agree on what I *will* do, we must also agree on what I *won't* do. Specifically, I need to promise God that I won't retaliate against those who offend me in the ways described earlier in this chapter: "Lord, to the best of my ability and with Your help, I will not snipe at coworkers who offend me. I will not enter into a cold war with them by withholding myself from them. I will not humiliate them, embarrass them, or put them down in any way. And I will not keep account of any wrongs I suffer."

Again, making such a promise doesn't guarantee perfection. But in making a commitment, you are inviting God to point out your failures and guide you back to the standard.

A helpful, practical way to solidify your commitments to God is to write them on index cards. Carry the cards in your pocket or purse and read them as prayers several times each day—especially before work begins. Keep the card handy at your work station for easy review through the day. You'll be amazed at how quickly God can transfer your commitment from a card to your heart and memory.

When Others Are Sniping at You

There are times when others at work may have a problem forgiving you for an intentional or unintentional offense. You will likely recognize the problem by their antagonistic behavior, as I did when Freida began sniping at me and when Gavin persisted in blasting George and me.

In many cases, a coworker's grudge is not primarily your problem. She has taken offense at something you said or did, perhaps something that was never intended to offend. But for whatever reason, the temperature between you has dropped to freezing. If the relationship is to return to a productive atmosphere, something must be done—and you must be ready to do it. Consider these guidelines for resolving a relationship in which someone else is holding a grudge against you.

Confront the issue. Once you are aware that some static exists between you and a coworker, get to the heart of the issue. Meet with the individual privately and say something like, "I'm concerned about our relationship. Have I offended you in some way?" Agreed: Confrontations are difficult, sometimes even painful. But don't let the issue slide by or try to cover over it. It will not get better, and it may get worse.

Invite openness. Encourage your offended coworker to unload his problem—and listen patiently as he does. Don't interrupt to try to justify yourself. Put yourself in his shoes and try to see the problem from his vantage point. Realize that there is no such thing as "it's all his problem." Be accepting, not judgmental.

Be ready to ask forgiveness. In whatever way you may have contributed to the negative situation, confess your offense and ask your coworker to forgive you. You may need to take the confrontation one step further by asking, "Is there something you want me to do that will help make things right?" As best you can, do what is necessary to clear the air and restore the relationship.

Being a giver and seeker of forgiveness among your fellow employees may be one of the most humbling, difficult disciplines you encounter as a believer. We don't like to admit our wrongs and failures, nor do we like to let others off the hook when they make mistakes. But being a minister of forgiveness where you work is one of the most powerful ways I know to gain the trust and respect of unbelieving coworkers. Your attitude and actions of humility in this area will open a wide door of opportunity for introducing your coworkers to the love and forgiveness of God.

· 9 ·

Keep an Open Mind

B Y ALL OUTWARD APPEARANCES, Jim was a living, breathing success story at Tektronix. He started with the company as a salesman and rapidly rose to a managerial position in the field. Once he moved to the factory, Jim ascended the ranks to occupy a series of high-level positions in operations. After 27 years with the company, Jim had tasted the fruits of success at every level of endeavor. But Jim had a problem: He had left countless numbers of enemies strewn along his pathway to success. Nearly everyone Jim had worked with during his career despised him.

Jim once told me his secret of "success." "Jerry, information is power," he said. And he believed it. Everywhere he went he carried a notebook stuffed with data on the operation of Tektronix. He could answer almost any question about the company and its policies. He used the information he accumulated to climb over people and get his way. He trusted no one and made himself vulnerable to no one. Instead, he stomped on anyone and everyone in his path to achieve his goals.

Eventually, Jim's heartless, blind ambition caught up with him. He made a mistake that people might forgive in anyone else. But for those whom he had offended along the way, Jim's misstep was the ammunition they needed to gun him down. Dozens of his victims from the past stepped out of the shadows to accuse him. As a result of the overwhelming tide against him, he was dismissed from his position and nearly blackballed from the company.

Jim was crushed. He thought he was doing well all

those years and didn't realize he had made so many enemies. Tektronix had been his life, and he wanted to stay with the company until retirement age. But he knew that if he didn't change, he would never find another job in the company. In light of his deep personal crises, Jim embarked on a season of self-examination and quietly made a genuine commitment to change.

As hard as Jim tried to convince the managers at Tek that he was different, nobody believed him—nobody except Maurice. Jim and Maurice had worked in the field together as salesmen in the old days. After learning of Jim's personal devastation and commitment to change, Maurice said, "I know Jim, and I know what he can do. I'm going to give him a chance." All the other managers warned Maurice against it. "Don't do it," they said. "He's bad news." But Maurice hired him anyway.

Shortly after that, Maurice, who was a friend of mine, came to work for me and brought Jim with him. "Wait a minute, Maurice," I protested. "I remember Jim. He has a bad rep in the company. I'm not sure I want him working in our organization." But Maurice assured me that Jim had changed his ways, so I reluctantly agreed to keep him on.

To the amazement of practically everyone who knew him—including me—Jim *had* changed. Over the next 2 years he exhibited an attitude of humility by serving his superiors and coworkers. I kept watching for the old negative patterns that had marked his behavior for 27 years, but they just weren't there anymore. I asked Jim to work for me and gave him greater levels of responsibility. He did a tremendous job, gradually gaining the respect of everyone in our division. And it all started when Maurice refused to buy into the popular opinion that Jim was bad news and that he would never change.

An Open Mind Is a Terrible Thing to Waste

One of the fastest ways to erode your trust and respect on the job is to respond to people and problems with a closed mind. You may tend to shrug off the detrimental aspects of this trait by calling yourself "opinionated" or "discriminating," but the issue is much more serious. We're really talking about judging individuals and circumstances before knowing all the facts, and that's prejudice. I don't know anyone who would be proud to be known as prejudiced in their dealings with coworkers. And I don't know anyone who would invest much trust or respect in a coworker who approached his work with a prejudiced attitude.

Responding to a situation or another person judgmentally takes very little effort, very little patience, and very little love. All you need to do is make some hasty declarations based on circumstantial evidence. That's what virtually all of us who knew Jim had done. However, responding to situations or people with discernment requires time, energy, patience, and love. Instead of closing the issue with definitive statements, you must open it up with probing questions, exposing it to the light of truth. Maurice is a beautiful example. He refused to join the lynch mob before investigating the facts about Jim. If it hadn't been for Maurice's patience and discernment, Jim may have ended up on Tek's scrap heap.

Solomon equated narrow-minded judgmentalism with foolishness and open-minded discernment with wisdom: "A simple man believes anything, but a prudent man gives thought to his steps" (Prov. 14:15). It is human nature to step up and judge. But the Holy Spirit's nature is to step back and discern. When you give the Holy Spirit time to help you investigate a situation or problem, you will likely respond to it helpfully instead of hurtfully. I'm not saying that every goldbrick or bad apple you work with will turn out like Jim. In reality, for everyone who makes a commitment to change and follows through as Jim did, there will be five who will not turn their lives around. But your commitment to approach such situations with patient discernment will maximize the positive possibilities and earn you the trust and respect of your coworkers regardless of the outcome.

False Judgments Based on Track Records

As in my experience with Jim, there are occasions when we judge people based on an extensive knowledge of their track record. In essence, this attitude says, "He's always been this way, and he will never change." In particular, there are several phrases we use that reflect judgmental thinking:

"He's never been able to do anything right." This was the rap on Bob, an engineering manager who once worked for me. Bob had been associated with several major projects and had done a very good job. But unfortunately, all of his projects were losers, failing miserably in the marketplace. In reality, the projects were ill-conceived before they got to Bob, and even his excellent work couldn't salvage their success. But Bob got the reputation that he couldn't produce a winner, and, subsequently, nobody wanted to hire him to engineer their projects.

Finally, another division manager gave Bob a thread of a chance. His division was working on three projects simultaneously. Two of them were grand and glorious computer systems that were supposed to make a big splash. The third project was called Nova, a rather small system that really wasn't expected to survive in the shadow of the other two "winners." "We can't expect much from Bob," the division heads agreed. "Let's give him Nova so that he can't hurt us too badly if he fails again." Bob was just thrilled to have a project and content to jump in and make it go.

The two big projects were afforded huge staffs of engineers, while Bob was assigned a skeleton crew for Nova. But both of the "big winners" fell behind schedule and eventually bombed in the marketplace because of technological failure. In the meantime, thanks to Bob's diligent work, Nova made it to the market on time and performed far above expectations.

Just because someone has a history of failure does not mean that he will always fail. That's closed-minded judgment, not open-minded discernment. He may fail again, and he may fail repeatedly. But if you withhold a future opportunity only on the basis of past failure, you may also be quenching a possible success.

"The facts don't lie." The problem with this assumption is that we may wrongly interpret a behavior as a fact. For example, your coworker often forgets to turn off his machine before leaving the office. You say, "He's irresponsible because he doesn't turn off his machine." However, irresponsibly failing to turn off a machine does not necessarily mean that your coworker is irresponsible. He may be responsible in many other areas, yet he just has trouble remembering to hit the off switch before leaving. If you brand him as irresponsible, you may be making a hasty, incorrect judgment that will block out future opportunities for him to prove himself responsible.

"You can't teach an old dog new tricks." Darrin was a technician at Tek who only interfaced with the marketing people when he was called in to answer technical questions for them. He had a real interest in marketing, but he didn't have the formal training. "If you want to get into marketing," his superiors responded to his requests for marketing tasks, "you need to go to school. Then you need to spend some time in the sales field. If you succeed in those areas, we may be able to give you a tryout here." Darrin's superiors really didn't believe a technician could make the transition to marketing.

Then a series of circumstances in Darrin's organization resulted in several marketing people quitting. Since Darrin was so eager and available, he was assigned a few marketing tasks to perform. He was an instant success, and the marketing department in his group suddenly came together. In fact, he did a much better job than the well-trained marketing people he replaced. During the next few years, Darrin became one of the top marketing people in the entire company. He eventually left Tek to become the senior marketing director for another corporation.

Darrin had an interest in marketing, but he had no

training, no credentials, and no experience. He wasn't about to get a chance from those who saw him only as a technician. Yet by breakdown and default he backed into an opportunity no one would offer him, and he became a star. Judgmentally locking a superior or subordinate into one field by saying, "That's the only thing he can do," may unnecessarily limit someone with great potential in other areas.

"She's always been a problem, and she always will be." Alicia was a very aggressive, assertive ladder climber in our company. She was hard and ruthless in her dealings with coworkers and was pigeonholed as an unyielding ramrod. Everybody steered clear of her.

Alicia was passed around the company like a hot potato because nobody believed she could handle the managerial role she was striving for. Finally, she ended up in my organization, but I was biased against her too. I really didn't believe she was capable of building a group of workers into a productive team. Not feeling very hopeful of succeeding with this "problem person," I took a deep breath and decided to take my best shot at helping her become a good manager.

I learned right away that there was much more to Alicia than her tough exterior revealed. When I confronted her about her irritating aggressive qualities, she admitted that she had developed a hard shell as a defense in order to survive in the dog-eat-dog business world. When I challenged her to quit beating everyone and everything into submission and assume the posture of a coach, Alicia accepted the challenge. She was thoroughly teachable. She threw away her tough exterior and began coaching her people instead of steamrolling them. All she needed was the guidance and encouragement that nobody had bothered to offer because she had been unfairly judged a perpetual problem.

False Judgments Based on Fragments of Evidence

Another way we wrongly leap to foolish judgment instead of exercising wise discernment is by building a case against people based on shreds of information and fragments of evidence. We're often guilty of this response when dealing with people we don't know well. For example, you hear a few coworkers say something in a meeting or observe a new boss's response in an isolated incident and make a judgment based on what little you've seen. "I've got him pegged," you say. "I've seen his kind before, and I know how he operates." The guy who challenges your idea at a meeting is branded a "troublemaker." The new girl who leaves the office five minutes early must be a "shirker." The coworker who invites the boss out to lunch is obviously an "apple polisher." Before you know it, you have fabricated a false identity or mind-set for someone that blocks out the truth about his real motives and abilities.

Raul, a division manager at Tek, was a sad example of jumping to judgments about people based on fragments of evidence. At one time, Raul headed up a critical project for the company that fell way behind. Everybody knew that Raul had set an unrealistic schedule for the project in light of his limited technological resources. But Raul was so blinded by his personal career wants and needs that he refused to dig in and find out what it would take to complete the project on time. Instead of admitting that it couldn't be done, he fired Wynn, his engineering manager, and hired Elliot to do the job.

Elliot innocently came on board eager to help and please his new boss. But after only a few weeks, he, too, was convinced that Raul's schedule and demands were unmeetable. "Your expectations are unrealistic," Elliot told Raul. "Your people don't have the experience to pull this off. You need some major technical breakthroughs for this to happen. We will never make your schedule."

Instead of discerning the truth in Elliot's evaluation, Raul reacted to him. "You're just like Wynn and the others," Raul said. "I know what I want, and if you can't do the job, good-bye." As soon as Elliot said it couldn't be done, Raul pegged him to be as incompetent as those who had "failed" before. Raul was blinded from the truth in the matter by his judgmentalism. He fired Elliot and brought in someone else who proved to be as "incompetent" as Elliot and Wynn.

Jumping to hasty judgments based on mere fragments of information will often block you from perceiving the truth about a fellow worker or a project. If you're going to be open-minded in your dealings at work, you must take the time and make the effort to gather sufficient information and discern the whole truth.

False Judgments Based on Binary Thinking

One of the great dangers to healthy open-mindedness in the workplace is our unwitting commitment to what I call binary thinking. Binary thinking is either/or, black-or-white thinking, the tendency to see only two options for a work situation, relationship, or problem. Binary thinking sees the truth at either one of two opposite poles: good/bad, right/wrong, for/against, me/you, we/they, with/without. There is no middle ground or gray area for the binary thinker. To be sure, for the Christian there are some issues in the work environment—particularly moral issues—that are clearly either right or wrong, good or bad. But there are other areas where we tend to overlook the possibilities for solutions in the middle by insisting that the answer lies at one end or the other.

Imagine, for example, that you and Angela are in charge of deciding which brand of photocopier to buy for the company. Your firm needs four machines, one for each floor. You recommend brand X because it features a color print model that is ideal for the third floor art department. But Angela insists on brand Y because they offer a machine that copies, collates, and staples reports at high speed, which the accounting department on the second floor needs. So you end up arm wrestling over which brand will best meet your company's needs.

Is it possible that the solution is somewhere in the middle instead of at one of the two poles? Must you deal exclusively with one copier manufacturer? Couldn't you recommend buying a brand X color machine for the first and third floors and a high-speed brand Y for floors two and four? Or perhaps the needs of the four floors would be best served by four different brands. Binary thinkers are so locked into black-or-white solutions that they cannot see the viable options and variations that may be lying between the poles. Open-minded discerners investigate every possibility along the continuum between what binary thinkers assume to be strictly either/or.

GUIDELINES FOR AN OPEN MIND

The Bible is very clear on the issue of judgment versus discernment. Closed-mindedness that leads to prejudice and hasty judgments is wrong. Open-mindedness that leads to thoughtful discernment and wise decisions is right. Again, this doesn't mean that there isn't a place for strategic closed-mindedness. We are to be closed-minded when faced with temptations to immorality, dishonesty, falsehood, etc. But the Christian in the workplace should be a leader in modeling open-mindedness and discernment among coworkers whom others are stifling through closed-minded judgment.

The following guidelines will help you apply the wisdom of Scripture to specific areas on the job where you need to demonstrate open-mindedness.

Take a close look at yourself. One of the best ways to keep from becoming judgmental is through consistent self-examination. When you are tempted to lash out at a coworker's weakness or failure, stop and take a good look at yourself. Those who rush to judge people and situations in the workplace often do so without realizing that they are capable—and sometimes even guilty—of committing the very behavior they condemn. That was the essence of Paul's message to the self-righteous Jews: "You, therefore, have no excuse, you who pass judgment on someone else, for at whatever point you judge the other, you are condemning yourself, because you who pass judgment do the same things" (Rom. 2:1). The New Testament repeatedly reminds us that the primary focus of our scrutiny and judgment is to be ourselves (Rom. 14:10; 1 Cor. 11:28, 31; 2 Cor. 13:5; Gal. 6:3-4). Frankly, if we followed these directives for self-examination faithfully, we wouldn't have time to judge others.

Whenever you are tempted to judge a coworker, transform that temptation into an opportunity for self-examination. For example, suppose you're in the lunchroom, and your fellow workers are cussing out the boss behind his back. Instead of pronouncing judgment on them for their behavior, ask yourself, "In what ways am *I* wrongly critical of the boss? Which of *my* attitudes and actions may be perpetuating the same hostility or lack of cooperation?" Or suppose you are ready to lambaste a coworker for taking some supplies from the storeroom for personal use. Stop and ask yourself, "Am *I* guilty of robbing the company in any way? Do *I* give the boss a full day's work for a full day's pay?" Honestly asking and answering knotty questions of self-scrutiny like these will keep the pressure on you to make changes where you really can: in yourself.

The priority of self-examination does not preclude the possibility that you may need to confront a coworker concerning his wrong behavior. But be sure you deal with yourself first in that area so that you can approach your coworker objectively instead of hypocritically.

Check the facts for accuracy. When you are tempted to string up a coworker for an apparent failure or impropriety, make sure you know the full story before you slam down the gavel of judgment on him. Remember: Closed-minded people make hasty judgments based on fragmentary, inconclusive evidence; open-minded people step back to allow time for the Holy Spirit to help them discern the issue. Jesus said, "Stop judging by mere appearances, and make a right judgment" (John 7:24). Paul instructed, "Test everything. Hold on to the good" (1 Thess. 5:21). The process of looking beyond appearances and testing the validity of "evidence" will keep you from a hasty, hurtful judgment.

Practically speaking, this means you must trace hearsay to the "horse's mouth," fine-tune generalities to facts, and dig under the surface to find the foundation. It also means you weigh opinion and biases—including your own—against hard data. Only after you have exposed "the truth, the whole truth, and nothing but the truth" are you in a position to discern and decide a course of action or follow through with a confrontation.

Expect change. If there ever was a man at Tek who tested my capacity to withhold judgment, it was Brad, who was my boss for a while. Brad had a terrible reputation for indecisiveness. Whenever a company issue came up that required him to make a decision, Brad just couldn't bring himself to make the call. He kept telling himself and his staff that he was going to quit dillydallying and be a decision maker. But when push came to shove, Brad was afraid to make a choice.

It would have been easy for me to brand him a spineless wimp. I was certainly tempted to. But God's grace helped me keep a positive attitude and try to help Brad change. Along with other members of the staff, I encouraged him toward decisiveness. "We're right behind you, Brad," we told him. "Whatever you decide is fine with us. We'll support you and help you make it happen." But no matter how much we communicated our belief in him and our encouragement, Brad wouldn't change. He eventually lost his job.

Most of the problem people you deal with at work probably aren't as bad off as Brad was. But if you convey through your words and actions that you don't believe they can change for the better, they likely won't change. Judgmental people are closed to the possibility of others changing. Discerning people leave room for God to work by expecting, encouraging, and praying for change in others.

If it hadn't been for an open-minded and discerning manager at Tektronix, I may not have succeeded as I did. Stan was my boss when I started as a technician. After I had been on the job about three weeks, Stan said, "Jerry, you have a mind for marketing. You belong in marketing, and I'm going to help you get there." I had no credentials in marketing, but Stan saw some abilities in me that no one else saw. He kept his word by grooming me for a marketing job, and my career at Tek took off.

Stan was known at the company as a manager who "grew" people. He had the uncanny ability to read people and their potential irrespective of their background, credentials, or education. He refused to judge or pigeonhole people, and his open-mindedness liberated people to grow. As a result, Stan was one of the most highly respected men in the company.

Think of what could happen where you work if an open-minded employee like Stan began seeing the best in his coworkers instead of stifling them through closed-minded judgmentalism. What is the possibility that *you* could be that person?

· 10 ·

Make Everyone Feel like Number One

EARLY IN MY MARKETING CAREER at Tek, I was assigned to a group developing a product called a scan converter, which is a tube designed to enhance a computer's display capabilities. The market was crying for our scan converter, but our laboratory was about 12 months behind in perfecting one of the components. In order to get our scan converter to market on time, our group decided to temporarily substitute a component from another reputable company for the one that was behind schedule. We planned to slide the Tek component into the converter as soon as it was perfected.

The substituted component was lower in performance compared to the one our engineers were working on, but it worked fine. I had done a lot of market research on our decision, and our customers were pleased with the prototype I showed them, even though it had a component from another company. We were ready to sell, and they were ready to buy. So I took our plan to a high level meeting for approval.

Being a junior marketing person addressing a roomful of corporate vice presidents, I was nervous. Had I realized who else would be attending the meeting, I would have been terrified. As I began my presentation, the back door opened, and in walked the last person I expected: Mr. Duvall, one of the most influential senior executives at Tek. Mr. Duvall rarely attended these kinds of meetings, but there he was, taking a seat in the back of the room. My heart leaped into my throat, and I continued to explain how we could take our scan converter to market early with the component from this other company.

After my presentation, Mr. Duvall began to question the validity of my research as the other company execs sat and listened. "They won't buy our scan converter," Mr. Duvall insisted. "That component is too low on performance." What I didn't know was that Mr. Duvall had a run-in with this company in the past, and he wasn't about to put one of their components in one of his products!

Somehow, my youthful enthusiasm and conviction suddenly got the best of me. "You don't know what you're talking about, Mr. Duvall," I retorted. "I've talked to all our big accounts, I've shown them the prototype, and they're ready to buy." Eyes widened and mouths dropped open in horror around the room. They couldn't believe that they had just heard a marketing nobody tell powerful Mr. Duvall that he didn't know what he was talking about.

Mr. Duvall didn't take kindly to being upstaged by a foot soldier in front of his lieutenants. He proceeded to verbally chew me up into little pieces and spit me out on the floor in front of everybody. He told me that I was naive and that I was the one who didn't know what I was talking about. At one point, Larry, our group VP, stood up and tried to intervene. "Sit down and shut up!" Mr. Duvall barked at him as he continued to give me the verbal blistering of my life. At Mr. Duvall's insistence, our scan converter would be delayed until our component was ready.

I was devastated. When I stumbled numbly out of the meeting, I knew my career at Tektronix was over. If Mr. Duvall didn't fire me, I was ready to quit. Suddenly, Larry was beside me with his arm draped over my shoulder. "It's OK, Jerry," he encouraged me warmly. "You did a good job. You're going to be all right. You're going to come out of this just fine."

Those few words saved my life at Tek. Larry made sure I knew he believed in me. And in those moments when I wasn't sure I believed in myself, his words meant everything to me. If Larry had failed to communicate his confidence in me, I might have walked away from a promising career and ministry opportunity. Without Larry's encouragement at a moment when I felt lower than a snake's belly, I wouldn't have lasted 23 years at Tek.

Six months later, our lab produced 10 sample converters, and we took 2,000 orders for them. But a few months later the lab announced that their technology had failed. They could come up with 10 working models, but they couldn't mass-produce them. We canceled the product, canceled the orders, and fought off two resulting lawsuits. Had we gone with the component from the other company as our group proposed, we would have been sitting pretty. But instead, our technological failure left our company in a financial mess and with a black eye in the computer electronics community.

Two years later, I happened to be seated next to Mr. Duvall at an awards banquet. My career at Tek was going very well. Mr. Duvall and I hadn't spoken since the day he chewed me out and delayed the scan converter project.

While we were eating, Mr. Duvall turned to me and said, "Jerry, you were right about that scan converter project." That's all he said. It was gratifying to be exonerated for the stand I took. But I felt an even deeper gratitude. If it hadn't been for Larry's timely words of encouragement, I might never have been at that banquet to hear Mr. Duvall's confession.

Timely Acknowledgment

The term I use to describe timely words and deeds of encouragement like Larry's is *acknowledgment*. To acknowledge a coworker means to notice, appreciate, and affirm him, not only as a worker but also as a person. Acknowledgment is an expression of concern, support, assistance, or protection for those you work with. Acknowledgment says, as Larry did to me, "It's OK. You did a good job. You're going to be all right. You're going to come out of this just fine."

As much as possible, we need to help our subordinates, peers, and superiors believe and feel that they are important to us. Obviously, not everyone you work with is your best friend or the number one performer in the company. Those roles are reserved for a select few. But everyone you work with has value, and acknowledgment is the ministry of recognizing each individual's unique value to you and contribution to the corporate endeavors. King Solomon admonished, "Do not withhold good from those who deserve it, when it is in your power to act" (Prov. 3:27). It should be the daily modus operandi of Christian employers and employees to find ways of injecting positive acknowledgment into the often negative environment of the worldly workplace.

There are many ways to acknowledge your coworkers, and I will highlight several of them in the paragraphs ahead. But first you need to understand a couple of important qualifiers that must be applied to every attempt at acknowledgment.

First, effective acknowledgment is unsolicited. If you only compliment and encourage your coworkers when they ask for it, they will begin to doubt their real value. Had Larry failed to encourage me that dark day until I asked, "Well, Larry, am I as great a failure as I think I am?" I couldn't have been sure if he was really acknowledging me or just saying something to placate me. The best expressions of comfort, affirmation, and encouragement are those that are offered freely. We must take the initiative to acknowledge others based on their need without waiting for them to request it.

Second, effective acknowledgment is sincere. Earlier we discussed the shallowness of flattery, and I want to underscore that here. If you don't mean it, don't say it. When a coworker blows an assignment, he needs acknowledgment from you. But if you say, "Great job!" just to make him feel good, he not only won't believe you but also won't appreciate you. You can acknowledge a coworker's effort or attempt sincerely without labeling his obvious failure a success.

Strategies for Acknowledging Coworkers

Here are seven specific strategies for ministering encouragement to the people you work with and thus increasing their sense of value as persons and workers:

Praise them publicly and privately. Perhaps the most direct means of acknowledging coworkers is through spoken praise: "You did a nice job on the Cochran account"; "I appreciate your willingness to stay late today so that I could get these orders filled"; "I noticed how you tried to help the customer even when he got belligerent about his reservation being mishandled"; "Your cheery smile and positive attitude really made my day"; "Thank you for letting me take an early lunch hour so that I could take my son to the dentist."

Sincere, praise-filled acknowledgments like these should generously spice your daily conversations on the job. You'll be amazed at how your positive, uplifting words will help create and maintain a positive, healthy atmosphere among your coworkers. Solomon recognized the great value of verbal praise when he wrote, "A word aptly spoken is like apples of gold in settings of silver" (Prov. 25:11). Words of praise are gifts that even the poorest employee can afford to distribute lavishly. In reality, we can't afford *not* to be generous with acknowledgments of spoken praise.

Sometimes words of praise should be private and personal: a face-to-face comment, a phone call, a brief interoffice memo, a note stuck on a file cabinet or lampshade, a card or letter, a message on the answering machine or computer monitor. At other times, praise should be public: singling out someone's contribution during a staff meeting, a positive comment about one coworker made to another, a note on the bulletin board or in the company newsletter, an informal comment in the lunchroom.

Words of praise, whether private or public, ought to be specific rather than general. When you say, "I appreciate you," add the word "for" and fill in the blank with a specific praiseworthy deed you observed personally: "for returning my calls so promptly"; "for reminding me to fill out my time card"; "for reducing my counseling load by taking two of my clients."

Offer positive correction. I've had numerous opportunities in my business career to take coworkers aside and lovingly say, "You need to know that you are the cause of a problem for other people. I'm only telling you this because I care about you and want to help you solve the problem." Though correction is often difficult to give and painful to receive, almost without exception these people have thanked me for caring enough to help them see a blind spot. In some cases, my words of correction prompted changes of behavior that helped someone avoid getting fired. Prov. 25:12 suggests that correction is as valuable as praise: "Like an earring of gold or an ornament of fine gold is a wise man's rebuke to a listening ear."

The key to correction's effectiveness is that it be offered positively with a view to helping people solve the problems they have created. You can't just go around telling people, "You messed up!" If you're going to correct someone, you must also be ready to say, "Here's what we can do to fix the problem." Positive correction is most meaningful when shared in private.

Give of your time. For most of us involved in gainful employment, time is a precious commodity. There always seems to be more task than time left at the end of the day. Everybody hoards his daily hours and minutes for his own responsibilities with little interest in expending them for someone else.

One of the most practical ways to acknowledge coworkers is to share some of your valuable time with them in order to make their tasks easier and their workday more successful. When you're on the time clock, time definitely is money. You cannot ignore your own responsibilities and just float around looking for other people's work to do. But when you invest a couple of minutes here and there to help someone carry some boxes to the storeroom, answer someone else's second line, cover a sick coworker's route, etc., you are showing how you value those individuals.

In a small company like FlightCom, which I once managed, it was easy for me to get stuck in my office all day doing a myriad of administrative tasks that kept the business machinery running. One day Alan and Jeanie urged, "Jerry, you need to walk through the production area more often just to show the people working out there that you are interested in them and what they're doing." They were right. Sometimes I would go for days without seeing any of the production people, even though their department was just a few steps from my office.

I took their advice to heart and began making the time each day to wander through production and talk to people. I was amazed at how positively people responded to my effort just to spend a few minutes with them at their workstations. I was also amazed at what the effort did for me. I gained a greater appreciation for my fellow workers and what they were doing as they assembled and shipped our intercoms and headsets. Before long, I really *wanted* to be out there with them. The time I spent in production was no longer a personal sacrifice; it was a personal pleasure.

We hear so much today about quality time versus quantity time. *Quality* is the key word. Quality without quantity is OK, but quantity without quality is definitely not OK. The amount of time we give to our coworkers, whether it be small or great, must qualitatively communicate their value to us.

Make yourself available. I'm thinking about those occasions when, instead of volunteering to give it, your time is demanded of you by someone who interrupts you. I used to think that the most efficient way to deal with people who needed my advice or help at an inopportune moment was to say, "Take a number; your request will be handled in the order in which it was received." But I have discovered that I consume less time in the long run if I drop what I'm doing and deal with the interrupting individual on the spot. Willingness to be available to coworkers this way also conveys how much you value them.

One afternoon I was busily pecking away at my computer keyboard on a FlightCom project when Alan rushed into my office. He started to ask me an important question when I cut him off abruptly. "Wait a second, Alan. I just remembered that I've got to return a call. I'll be with you as soon as I'm done with the call." Alan turned and walked out of my office without completing his question.

I was on the phone for about 15 minutes. Then, forgetting all about Alan, I went back to the computer. Half an hour later, I remembered. I shot out of my chair and into Alan's office. He had been unable to proceed on his task until he had a reply from me. As it turned out, it took me about a minute to answer his question. He'd been dead in the water for 45 minutes because I was "too busy" to give him 1 minute!

Solomon has a poignant instruction about making ourselves available: "Do not say to your neighbor, 'Come back later; I'll give it tomorrow'—when you now have it with you" (Prov. 3:28). One of the greatest examples of this verse I have ever known was a project manager at Tek. Dave was extremely successful at building a team and getting a project done because he was committed to availability. Once he told his team, "I don't care where I am or what I'm doing, even if I'm in a meeting with the president of the company—if you need me, you can come get me." When your coworkers know that you are imminently interruptible to help them, you will communicate that they are of great value to you.

Be a good listener. Merle was a marketing man at Tek who worked for me for eight years. Every person who came to talk to Merle about a project or problem walked away feeling as if he was somebody. That's how I felt whenever I talked with him. Merle was one of the most attentive listeners I've ever known. He was a master at showing interest by asking questions about the subject. Merle always made me feel that what I was telling him was the most important information he'd ever heard.

A good listener communicates value to those who are speaking to him. There are many listening skills that tell others, "Keep talking; I'm all ears." First, give your full attention to listening by stopping whatever else you're doing. You may be able to listen effectively while you type, draw, stock shelves, or lick stamps. But when you are busy with another task, others perceive that you are not listening. Give them 100 percent attention when they speak to you.

Second, facial expression and eye contact are important. Prov. 15:30 says: "A cheerful look brings joy to the heart." If you *are* interested, but you don't *look* interested, the speaker will think you're not interested. But if you *look* interested—pleasant, inviting expression, eye-to-eye contact, smile, occasional nod—the speaker will believe that you really *are* interested.

Third, interaction and response conveys interested listening. When you interject comments that show that you are tracking with the conversation, and when you ask pertinent questions that invite the speaker to "tell me more," you are expressing value in him and what he has to say. Even your voice tone and inflection in your response can convey your interest.

Reach out and touch. Once, two of my former business partners—Jack and Mike—were meeting with me to interview a prospective employee. Since these two men were my brothers in Christ as well as my partners, when Jack and Mike arrived for the meeting, we embraced each other as we usually did when we got together. Our interviewee sat and watched wide-eyed. "You guys really love each other, don't you?" she said with amazement. Our nonverbal physical expression communicates volumes of information about how we value each other.

Acknowledging coworkers through touch openly conveys value and love. You may not feel free to greet everyone in the office or plant every day with a full-blown embrace, and it may not be an appropriate expression in some cases. But you can convey affirmation, acceptance, and encouragement through a friendly handshake, a gentle hug, a squeeze of the elbow, a pat on the back, etc. Whatever you do, just be sure your loving touch is free of anything that could be construed as an inappropriate sexual advance or suggestion.

Share your needs. Perhaps one of the most difficult ways for you to acknowledge the value of your coworkers is to open yourself up to them by sharing your personal needs. I'm not saying that you should publish your weaknesses and problems in the company newspaper. But there are some coworkers to whom you can convey value by confiding, "I'm hurting; I need your advice, I need your support." When you make yourself vulnerable in this way, you are saying, "I trust you," and giving others the opportunity of ministering to your needs and trusting you with their needs.

But beware. By becoming vulnerable to others, you lay yourself wide open to the possibility of being hurt, betrayed, and ridiculed. Instead of responding positively to your openness, some coworkers may use your confessions of need to discredit you to others in order to advance their own causes. That's the price of vulnerability. Ask God to show you those in your workplace who will most be uplifted and encouraged by your expressions of openness, and trust Him to protect you from those who might use your openness against you.

Acknowledgment: A Gift or a Discipline?

Janice, who worked for me for a while, had an uncanny sense for acknowledgment. She always seemed to be tuned in to our coworkers and alert to opportunities to affirm and encourage them. Janice would come into my office every couple of days and say something like, "Did you know that Toby was here late Friday night and most of Saturday solving that software problem? You need to go talk to him today and express your thanks for his extra work." She kept me on my toes by reminding me of the importance of valuing our coworkers for both their ordinary and extraordinary contributions.

There are those people like Janice who have a sense for acknowledgment. They're more in tune with people and their needs. Other people, like me, don't have the gift of acknowledgment, so we must develop the skill through personal discipline. I often get so wrapped up in products and processes that I sometimes overlook the people who make the products and processes work. I need to constantly remind myself to recognize all those people around me, help me reach my goals.

If you're more like me than like Janice, you need to develop the discipline of acknowledgment to make up for your lack of sensitivity to people. Write notes reminding yourself to spend time acknowledging those around you each week. Mark the birthdays and anniversaries of your coworkers on your calendar, and discipline yourself to send them a card, buy them a simple gift, or take them to lunch. As you develop the discipline of acknowledgment, you will find that it will sharpen your sense for affirming people.

Giving Is More Important than Receiving

That's all well and good, Jerry, you may be thinking. But I need encouragement too. If I spend all my time and energy acknowledging others, who is going to acknowledge and affirm me?

Yes, we all need encouragement, affirmation, and recognition. And it's nice when others come alongside, as Larry did for me, to bolster our morale by conveying that we are important to them. But the Bible clearly instructs us not to go out campaigning for people to acknowledge us, but to focus on pleasing God and others. Paul instructed: "Each of us should please his neighbor for his good, to build him up" (Rom. 15:2); "Do nothing out of selfish ambition or vain conceit, but in humility consider others better than yourselves" (Phil. 2:3). Our assignment as Christian workers is to put others first, not ourselves.

The penalty for trying to be first in the eyes of others is

to be last in the eyes of God. When we are centered on seeking the recognition of people, we are excluding ourselves from being recognized by God. Jesus said, "How can you believe if you accept praise from one another, yet make no effort to obtain the praise that comes from the only God?" (John 5:44). Paul wrote, "Am I now trying to win the approval of men, or of God? Or am I trying to please men? If I were still trying to please men, I would not be a servant of Christ" (Gal. 1:10).

But the reward of being last in the eyes of others is to be first in the eyes of God. When I make it a priority to acknowledge others instead of seek acknowledgment for myself, I sense the Holy Spirit acknowledging me. I believe this inner affirmation is the direct result of following the Bible's formula for acknowledgment: "Humble yourselves, therefore, under God's mighty hand, that he may lift you up in due time" (1 Pet. 5:6); "Seek first his kingdom and his righteousness, and all these things will be given to you as well" (Matt. 6:33); "Give, and it will be given to you. A good measure, pressed down, shaken together and running over, will be poured into your lap. For with the measure you use, it will be measured to you" (Luke 6:38).

God's recognition, affirmation, and encouragement are infinitely more rewarding than any kudos we may receive from our coworkers. They are substantial and eternal—the difference between "gold, silver, costly stones" that endure and "wood, hay or straw" that perish (1 Cor. 3:12). Our choice is to seek recognition from others and live with whatever we can accumulate, or seek recognition from God by acknowledging others and experience the abundance of His acknowledgment now and throughout eternity. In that light, it doesn't seem like much of a choice, does it?